Healing Conversations Now: Enhance Relationships With Elders and Dying Loved Ones

Joan W. Chadbourne and Tony Silbert

Taos Institute Publications
Chagrin Falls, Ohio

Healing Conversations Now:
Enhance Relationships With Elders and Dying Loved Ones

Copyright © 2011 Taos Institute Publications

All rights reserved.

COVER DESIGN: Kris Harmat

Library of Congress Catalog Card Number: 2011922000

Taos Institute Publications
A Division of the Taos Institute
Chagrin Falls, Ohio
USA

ISBN-10: 0-9819076-7-9
ISBN-13: 978-0-9819076-7-3   Printed in the USA and in the UK

Taos Institute Publications

The Taos Institute is a nonprofit organization dedicated to the development of social constructionist theory and practice for purposes of world benefit. Constructionist theory and practice locate the source of meaning, value, and action in communicative relations among people. Our major investment is in fostering relational processes that can enhance the welfare of people and the world in which they live. Taos Institute Publications offers contributions to cuttingedge theory and practice in social construction. Our books are designed for scholars, practitioners, students, and the openly curious public. The **Focus Book Series** provides brief introductions and overviews that illuminate theories, concepts, and useful practices. The **Tempo Book Series** is especially dedicated to the general public and to practitioners. The **Books for Professionals Series** provides in-depth works, that focus on recent developments in theory and practice. Our books are particularly relevant to social scientists and to practitioners concerned with individual, family, organizational, community, and societal change.

Kenneth J. Gergen
President, Board of Directors
The Taos Institute

Taos Institute Board of Directors

Books for Professional Series Editor
Kenneth Gergen

Tempo Series Editor
Mary Gergen

Focus Book Series Editors
Jane Seiling and Jackie Stavros

Executive Director
Dawn Dole

For information about the Taos Institute and social constructionism
visit: www.taosinstitute.net

Taos Institute Publications

Taos Tempo Series:
Collaborative Practices for Changing Times

Healing Conversations Now: Enhance Relationships With Elders and Dying Loved Ones, (2011) by Joan W. Chadbourne & Tony Silbert

Riding the Current: How to Deal with the Daily Deluge of Data, (2010) by Madelyn Blair

Ordinary Life Therapy: Experiences from a Collaborative Systemic Practice, (2009) by Carina Håkansson

Mapping Dialogue: Essential Tools for Social Change, (2008) by Marianne "Mille" Bojer, Heiko Roehl, Mariane Knuth-Hollesen, & Colleen Magner

Positive Family Dynamics: Appreciative Inquiry Questions to Bring Out the Best in Families, (2008) by Dawn Cooperrider Dole, Jen Hetzel Silbert, Ada Jo Mann, & Diana Whitney

Focus Book Series

The Appreciative Organization, Revised Edition (2008) by Harlene Anderson, David Cooperrider, Ken Gergen, Mary Gergen, Sheila McNamee, Jane Watkins, & Diana Whitney

Appreciative Inquiry: A Positive Approach to Building Cooperative Capacity, (2005) by Frank Barrett & Ronald Fry

Dynamic Relationships: Unleashing the Power of Appreciative Inquiry in Daily Living, (2005) by Jacqueline Stavros & Cheri B. Torres

Appreciative Sharing of Knowledge: Leveraging Knowledge Management for Strategic Change, (2004) by Tojo Thatchekery

Social Construction: Entering the Dialogue, (2004) by Kenneth J. Gergen, & Mary Gergen

Appreciative Leaders: In the Eye of the Beholder, (2001) edited by Marge Schiller, Bea Mah Holland, & Deanna Riley

Experience AI: A Practitioner's Guide to Integrating Appreciative Inquiry and Experiential Learning, (2001) by Miriam Ricketts & Jim Willis

Books for Professionals Series

For on-line ordering of books
from Taos Institute Publications visit
www.taosinstitutepublications.net

For further information, call:
1-888-999-TAOS, 1-440-338-6733
Email: info@taosinstitute.net

Table of Contents

Acknowledgments

We wish to extend gratitude to all of those who have encouraged and championed us and to the many who have told their stories. We will name only a few who have given specific support.

Joan's writing group gave on-going feedback from the very beginning. Members have been thinking partners and story advocates through so many revisions. They nurtured and nudged in the most helpful of ways; they also added essential stories. Meg Weston generously facilitated and created the group. Her expertise and gentle comments guided this book. Katherine Greenleaf asked incredibly thought-provoking questions; she instigated many helpful re-writes that made the book better. Patricia M. Amidon listened with a reader's ear and enthusiastically shared stories that wonderfully illustrated points important to this work. Kathleen Palmer's sensitive presence and stories along with her writing skill added another dimension.

Many have shared their writing and technical expertise. Their many gifts are very much appreciated. Thanks go to: Ari Barkan, Julie Barnes, Sam Clannon, Bob Cotter, Dawn Dole,

Marcia Feller, Louise Flynt, Mary Gergen, Roz Gerst, Tanya (Silbert) Henningsen, Jessie James, Jackie Kelm, Ann Landsberg, Kathleen Luke, Ada Jo Mann, Jean Mattimore, Patricia Matteo, Ashley St. Pierre, Marge Schiller, Jen Hetzel Silbert, Maggie Taylor, and Peter Whitehouse.

There would be no book without the many who shared stories. Thank you for opening your hearts and lives to contribute your experiences. Patricia Amidon, Patricia Bartke, Kaye Chatterton, Jack Cole, Yaeko Collins, Marcia Feller, Beth Fitzgerald, Roz Gerst, Katherine Greenleaf, Nancy Hohmann, Lynn D. Johnson, Roz Kay, Bobbi Keppel, Darlena Lake, Jane Lake, Marguerite Lawn, Jean Mattimore, Lucille Meltz, Alan Mong, Mary Lou Page, Kathleen Palmer, Joan Peet, Marvis Rodrigues, Rob Voyle, and Mariam Weidner.

We appreciate the contributions all of you have made to this book.

With Love,
Joan and Tony

Dedicated with Gratitude

Joan's Gratitude and Honor to:

My father, Earl Warrington, who was the first to show me how to die with dignity, how to face the end with equanimity, and how to make decisions to live fully until it is time to die, then doing so calmly and peacefully.

My mother, Rose Vittes Warrington, who let go of her rage as she approached the end of her life, which allowed me to experience exquisite connectedness. She gave a gift of grace. Living in the space of pure love for the last three months of her life opened my heart and taught me what is possible among spirit beings.

Omar, whose companionship reminded me of the joy, tenderness, and sense of oneness that is available when we open our hearts to each other. We shared a field of love beyond ego or personality differences that was most vibrant at the end of his life. He showed me the connectedness of all beings.

The loved ones who have passed taught me a lot about opening my heart, love, and dying. However, I must acknowledge my Aunt Eva (Vittes). Our engagement in Healing Conversations over the past thirteen years, my longest standing conversation with an elder, has laid the foundation for understanding the value, form, and purpose of Healing Conversations. She has been my greatest teacher. She has allowed me to ask questions, hear stories, and come to realizations that are essential to this work. She certainly reminds me that the time is NOW to begin Healing Conversations with our elders.

Tony's Gratitude and Honor to:

My mom, Lynne Silbert, who opened the door to Healing Conversations. This book was conceived during my mom's journey with cancer. I celebrate Mom for always being there for me, her ever-positive outlook on life, her warmth and friendliness, and for her courage and strength throughout. I miss you, but as my daughter, Bree, reminds me, anytime we want to see Me-Me, we can look to the stars.

My dad, Arnold Silbert, whom I had my first healing conversation with after my grandmother passed away. I'm thankful that we now live closer and can spend more time together. I look forward to many more healing conversations with you. I love you.

My wife (Jen) and daughters (Brianna and Jocelyn), who love me every day. Jen for being my partner in life, and for your strength, encouragement, and always putting family first. To my girls, for their smiles, hugs, and kisses whenever I need them. For your fresh and unassuming perspective on aging and death, you remind me it is only when we get older that death seems scary. I also appreciate you all sharing some of your nights and weekends with Joan and me.

Joan, my co-author and companion on this journey to create the book. Healing Conversations Now would still just be a twinkle in my eye, instead of what you are about to read. I'm truly grateful for the time, energy, passion, effort, and determination you gave to bring this book to life. Your wisdom, intuition, and insights are amazing. Our own healing conversations throughout this journey, not only strengthened our relationship; they made the book even better.

The Appreciative Inquiry community, in my moment of need I reached out to you, and what an amazing response. The outpouring of support, questions, resources, and stories was incredible. The generosity of this community continues to inspire, surprise, and delight me. Thanks for showing me how important this topic is to so many, and for planting the seeds for this book to grow.

Healing Conversations Now: Enhance Relationships With Elders and Dying Loved Ones

Introduction

Imagine knowing someone for most of your life, then, after years, discovering that person was so much more complex and interesting than you ever realized. As you listen to that person's life stories, you are surprised and delighted by the intriguing experiences and valuable insights that he or she shares. As you come to know each other better, you both gain an appreciation of your own and the other's life and develop closer bonds. The relationship between you becomes more satisfying as shown in the following personal anecdotes.[1]

> My Uncle Max was the eccentric one in the family. Quiet, slow of speech, and gnome-like, he was easy to overlook.

---

1 Most of the stories in this book are based directly on storytellers' reports. The first two story tidbits in this section are compiled from the essence of various stories. The second two are the author, Joan Chadbourne's, true stories.

No one knew much about him. One day, I asked him what accomplishment he was most proud of. His extraordinary story took me by surprise.

Uncle Max revealed the perseverance, resiliency, and ingenuity it took to unravel one of the fundamental chemical processes in manufacturing nylon. For the first time, I saw him through new eyes; I had underestimated him. My unassuming uncle had contributed to society in a way I would never have guessed.

That conversation was a gift. It was my uncle's gift to me – a gift of awareness, revelation, and quiet pride. My gift to him was to hear, to understand, and to see him anew.

⚊⚬⚊

My paternal grandmother was a favorite of mine. When I was a child, she listened to my stories for hours. I appreciated her attention and caring. She was always the loving Bubbie in my mind. It was not until decades later, when I began asking her questions about her life, that I began to see her more fully.

She disclosed that she, too, loved to write, and she eagerly shared some of her writing with me. I was spellbound reading her unpublished literary essays. She was obviously well read. I appreciated her in new ways. We began an expanded relationship with each other. We talked about our writing and encouraged each other.

Thank heavens my curiosity urged me to engage with her in a new way. I'd never have known what I missed if I'd continued to relate to Bubbie as nothing more than the loving grandmother who listened. Our relationship became adult-to-adult and more valuable.

—————•—•—————

My father never said much during nightly family dinners. It seemed he deferred to my mother to make decisions. I judged him as quite complacent and passive. During my childhood I paid little attention to him, assuming we didn't have much in common.

My perceptions changed when he allowed me to journey with him during his last year, following a terminal diagnosis. When I took time to be with him, often in silence, I discovered the gifts he had to offer.

He showed me a way to face one of life's greatest challenges, death, with dignity, courage, and decisiveness. When we told him cancer had spread to his brain and asked how he wanted to spend the rest of his time, he was clear. He asked me to take care of my mother and take care of the CD that was due twelve days later. He asked to be taken home, and he stopped eating.

Our conversations then became mostly silent and powerful. He lay peacefully holding my hand. He showed no fear, only acceptance. He was ready for death. Eight days after the final diagnosis, he died peacefully while my mother and I held his comforting hands. He taught me one of my most valued life lessons and changed my relationship to death forever. I am no longer afraid; I saw how to die well and am forever grateful to him.

—————•—•—————

As a much-wanted only child, my bond with my mother was always strong. However, periodically she raged, sometimes at me. Her voice was so shrill I'd recoil and go numb. I became speechless and felt helpless when she attacked. Over time, I grew a protective shell that kept distance between us.

In her eighties, she contracted brain cancer and was no longer capable of caring for herself. I became her primary caregiver. She could speak only a few words, yet her eyes said it all. When I'd walk into the room or do something for her, her love was as delightful as the sweet scent of another's perfume. She didn't resist her situation or her need to be cared for; instead, she smiled with gratitude.

In those last months, a miraculous shift happened. I call it grace. She could have become angrier, considering her deteriorated condition. Instead, the rage disappeared and there was no longer any need to protect myself from it. Together we experienced a pure, unquestioning love. The quality of that love showed me what was possible and enticed me to open my heart to more intimate relationships. We healed the distance between us. I am grateful that I was able to hear and see the shift and accept her love.

These story snippets describe the kinds of discoveries and shifts people have made as they've engaged in Healing Conversations. Some of these conversations were planned and some spontaneous. Some involved appreciative questions and stories, and some were silent but powerful interactions. They are examples of what is possible when we connect with compassion and curiosity. This book contains many stories of what happens when people engage in Healing Conversations, and we hope they inspire you to engage in similar explorations.

This book is also a handbook that provides the essentials needed so that you can engage in satisfying conversations. Using the approach and suggestions in this book will prepare you to enter into Healing Conversations. We share the types of questions, appreciative and energetic, and the distinctive quality of listening, connected listening, which will invite elders and dying loved ones into these different and more meaningful conversations. Beginning with a plan and structure will enable you to be comfortable initiating these interactions. Over time, they are likely to become more spontaneous.

The process of Healing Conversations will enhance any relationship. However, in this book we focus on intergenerational conversations with elders and dying loved ones. We've chosen this focus because many have told us how difficult it is to engage in meaningful conversations with their elder loved ones. Many do not know where to start. We hope this book helps.

HEALING FROM DIS-EASE: TWO AT A TIME

In the context of Healing Conversations, healing does not mean physical recovery so much as emotional, interpersonal, spiritual, and personal well-being. Healing is a process of becoming more whole and connected. Even if we're physically weak, our sense of well-being expands as we find peace and acceptance with our situation.

As many of the stories in this book demonstrate, people experience love, connection, and peace as they engage, build trust, and open themselves to each other in new ways. These enhanced relationships can happen even as a person declines physically. In fact, the urgency of death often amplifies the quality of Healing Conversations and their ability to bring comfort and connection. These connections facilitate peace and acceptance even if not physical healing.

What do people heal from as a result of Healing Conversations? Separation and isolation is our answer. In this culture, we have exalted rugged individuals who supposedly pull themselves up by their bootstraps. They are independent and don't need anyone. The result of this cultural myth is a pervasive sense of being alone, separate, and isolated.

The degree of isolation we feel determines life satisfaction, especially as we age. Research on aging correlates greater social interaction with improved health and vitality. Studies show that when people interact with others their sense of well-being increases. They take fewer medications and live longer.[2] The core dis-ease, isolation, is healed.

Many believe that our sense of being "bounded" creates isolation. Kenneth Gergen describes the concept of the bounded self, the individual within his or her skin. He writes, "You are there within your shell, and I am here within mine."[3] We are separate and responsible for everything that happens to us. We value our unique identities. In contrast, he describes the relational being as a person embedded in a web of inter-dependent relationships. In that context, we recognize that everything we do is built upon others' contributions.

We acknowledge many paths to healing, but in this book we describe a relational one. When we feel linked with another, we expand and go beyond the isolated and bounded self. We come to life, feel vital, and more whole. It takes two or more to create this path.

2 Lyubomirsky, S. The How of Happiness: A Scientific Approach to Getting the Life You Want. The Penguin Press, NY: 2008. Pg 195-197.
3 Gergen, K. Relational Being: Beyond Self and Community. Oxford University Press, NY: 2009.

WHY THIS BOOK?

The authors' own lives changed as we had conversations with aging and dying loved ones. The resulting enriched relationships added to our lives, and we are grateful. The conversations were powerful and changed us. New and more promising understandings of aging, death, and ourselves were an added bonus.

In retrospect, asking affirmative questions and listening to life stories is an obvious thing to do with our elders. Yet, we didn't engage in such conversations until we faced the deaths of our parents. Years later we realized that when we began asking energizing questions and listening to life stories, we learned so much about our loved ones and ourselves. Our relationships shifted. They became more loving and intimate. We were delighted with the results, and we wanted to share the stories, the questions, and the process. Hopefully others will strengthen relationships with their loved ones by using these tools. We defined the essential elements of those conversations and a process we could share with others, calling it "Healing Conversations."

When we began talking about Healing Conversations with others, people were so eager to share their stories that they often jumped in before we had an opportunity to finish ours. Many told of special relationships they had developed with elder loved ones. Some were sad because they hadn't spent more time in meaningful conversations before it was too late. The stories were heartwarming and confirming. We decided to publish a book that shares stories of these conversations and provides tools so that you can comfortably engage in Healing Conversations with people in your own life.

FOUNDATIONS OF HEALING CONVERSATIONS

Underlying Healing Conversations is the philosophy and framework of Appreciative Inquiry (AI). AI was originally created for organizational analysis, planning, and change. However, the spirit of Appreciative Inquiry is one of inquiry, learning, and discovery.[4] Awe and wonder are part of the process when people come together to share knowledge, listen to one another's stories, and create together. It honors and values all voices. Its methodology is one of asking questions and listening in a connected way. Doing so generates new possibilities. Inquiries usually ask for responses in story form. We have adapted this process to Healing Conversations, which has many applications for

4 Cooperrider, D., F. Barrett. "An Exploration of the Spiritual Heart of Human Science Inquiry. "Cleveland, OH: Case Western Reserve University, 2001.

families, couples, and intergenerational relationships.

It is not necessary to understand Appreciative Inquiry fully before engaging in satisfying Healing Conversations of your own. However, knowing the basics of its philosophy and methodology will enhance your ability to create your own energizing and appreciative questions. You'll be equipped to be more present, spontaneous, confident, and successful.

There are two bodies of research underlying Appreciative Inquiry that explain how and why Healing Conversations work: Positive psychology and social constructionism.

Positive psychology offers three main ideas, which support Healing Conversations: (1) Positively framed questions result in appreciative and inspiring stories. Sharing these appreciative stories generates connections and positive emotions. (2) Positive emotions create upward spirals of thought, action, and behavior. They can undo lingering negative emotions, and they can increase resiliency over time. Positivity fosters the ability to see more options.[5] (3) A focus on discovering strengths, values, and hopes for the future creates positive energy and a sense of accomplishment. This focus helps people appreciate what they have accomplished and acknowledge their worth.

---

5 Fredrickson, B. L. (2001). The role of positive emotions in positive psychology: The broaden-and-build theory of positive emotions. American Psychologist, 56, 218-226.

The other scientific perspective, social constructionism, refers to relational ways of knowing and making sense of the world. As it relates to Healing Conversations, there are two important concepts: (1) Together, we co-create our understanding of the world, which is subjective. It is not what is "out there," but our interpretation of events that creates what we think of as reality. We make meaning of our experiences in relationships through conversation and dialogue. (2) Our words create our worlds. Not only do we co-construct our understanding and meaning of the world, we actively shape the world we see, through our conversations. Our stories become our reality. As we recognize the many potential versions of any story, we see more possibilities and options.[6]

A WORD ABOUT CONVERSATION PARTNERS

One person hopes for a closer relationship and sees that possibility. That person is curious and wants to know the other better or to mend a rift or to support the other. That person initiates conversation by asking questions about the best of the other person's life, what's important to that person. We will call

6 Gergen, K. J. & Mary Gergen. Social Construction: Entering the Dialogue. Chagrin Falls, OH: A Taos Institute Publication. 2004.

the curious person by several names – none of them adequate to fully describe that person's contribution to the conversation. We will use the terms conversation-starter, initiator, listener, and when writing of conversations after a serious diagnosis or at end of life we may call this person, caregiver.

Initiators ask energizing questions, listen, connect, and reflect on what they've heard. They are present, curious, and compassionate. As they listen to the story they reflect and may ask clarifying questions. They extend an open hand to the other, hoping the other will take that hand, so they can journey together.

Elder, loved one, and storyteller are terms we use to refer to the person who the initiator invites to tell his or her story. That person might be anyone the conversation starter wants to know better. In this book, it is an elder unless a dying loved one is a younger person. When we talk about dying loved ones we may also use the term patient.

STRUCTURED AND SPONTANEOUS HEALING CONVERSATIONS

Language cannot adequately describe what happens in Healing Conversations, yet those involved feel it. As conversation partners explore experiences together, they create a shared sense of meaning and relationship. They feel closer and less alone.

The process is a dynamic one. Storytellers also listen. They hear their stories differently when they share them with another person. Both people gain perspective and learn from one another. As loved ones share their stories and initiators listen appreciatively, mutual trust increases. Relationships grow more intimate and satisfying.

In this book are examples of structured and spontaneous Healing Conversations. The kinds of questions, quality of listening, and storytelling are the same. The difference is that in the planned conversations, initiators prepare for the interaction. They choose topics of interest and then create supporting, energizing, and appreciative questions to explore those topics. They are selected because they are likely to elicit the kind of stories and information the listener wants to learn more about. These stories are also likely to remind storytellers of their rich and valuable lives. Many initiators write a list of questions and possible follow-up inquiries. They use what they have prepared during the conversation.

Preparation allows initiators to create a flexible "map." We travel as we would on a trip. The route may shift as unexpected situations emerge. We take detours for road construction, or may explore a new road that intrigues us. The map designates where to begin and how to proceed; the journey between these two destinations will vary. Structured Healing Conversations bridge the gap from not knowing what to say, to easily engaging in more spontaneous interactions.

Spontaneous conversations happen after the conversation-starter masters the basic elements: appreciative and energizing questions, storytelling, and connected listening. With practice these fundamentals come easily; initiators are able to listen and form questions in the moment. When both people are comfortable with these kinds of questions and storytelling, the structured process fades away. It is similar to building the foundation of a house. Forms create the desired shape, and when that shape is in place, the forms are no longer necessary.

MANY APPLICATIONS OF THE HEALING CONVERSATIONS PROCESS

Although we defined the process, principles, and skills of Healing Conversations in the context of relating to our dying and elder loved ones, we recognize the power they hold to enhance any relationship. Elders could initiate such conversations with their family members and caregivers. When Tony and Jen were dating they had a Healing Conversation to explore their individual dreams. They discovered shared hopes and wishes. The result was an engagement, satisfying marriage, and a growing family. We imagine families having similar conversations around the dinner table. We have used a comparable process in organizations and communities.

In other words, the principles and methods of Healing Conversations are applicable to anyone who wants to enhance relationships. When people engage in Healing Conversations they build webs of connection that benefit individuals, families, groups, organizations, and communities. The form remains the same. The topic and content of questions need to be tailored to the relationship and situation.

HOW TO READ THIS BOOK

The book is written for all readers who want better relationships with their elders or dying loved ones. You may decide to read it when you realize you'd like a more meaningful relationship with an elder, or you may choose it when a loved one is dying and you want to know what to do and say. The main point of the book is building, enhancing, and mending relationships through conversations.

The book has two sections: Section 1: Healing conversations: Getting to Know Them Better to Loving Them Goodbye and Section 2: Healing Conversations: The Essentials, Preparation, and Mastery.

Section 1: Healing Conversations: Getting to Know Them Bettter to Loving Them Goodbye (Chapters 1 – 7). Each of these chapters begins with stories that illustrate possibilities for more satisfying relationships through conversations. At the end of each chapter is a list of questions (conversation starters) for each kind of Healing Conversation.

Each chapter in this section covers key conversations: Getting to Know them Better, Enhancing and Mending Relationships, Finding Peace and Acceptance, Creative and Positive Aging, Conversations After a Serious Diagnosis, and Loving them Goodbye.

Some will read the stories and accompanying material to discover what is possible. They may look for inspiration and hope for more satisfying interactions. They may only skim the questions section until they are about to initiate conversations.

Some readers will go directly to the questions and suggestions at the end of each chapter. They may go to our website for even more questions. They want to jump right into conversations. The suggested questions reflect the approach and philosophy of Healing Conversations, and it makes a difference. If readers feel a sense of urgency, we suggest they read the questions and at least chapters 8 and 9 in Section 2 so that they have the tools necessary for spontaneous conversations.

Either process will work although reading the stories may broaden readers' appreciation of what is possible and provide nuances that influence how conversations unfold. If readers begin with questions, they can always return to the stories if they want more or if they get stuck.

Section 2: Healing Conversations: The Essentials, Preparation, and Mastery (Chapters 8 – 11) does exactly what it says. It provides detailed information about the foundational building blocks of Healing Conversations and how to prepare for, and master, the skills needed to engage in Healing Conversations more comfortably. This foundation helps readers to understand the dynamics of any kind of conversation. Having these basics gives many initiators the confidence to begin, and the skills to deal with whatever emerges. Once the basics are a natural part of the initiator's repertoire he or she can create new questions in the moment.

Chapter 8 outlines the essential building blocks: appreciative, energizing questions and stories. The format of the question is a core element of Healing Conversations and makes all the difference in the quality of the conversation. Learning to naturally craft questions that seek the best of the past will energize the conversation and the people involved.

Chapter 9 highlights the 1, 2, 3's of Healing Conversations. They are intention, presence, and connected listening. The quality of presence and listening is the core of the "healing" part of these conversations. Intention shapes the focus of the conversation, enhancing the relationship.

Chapter 10 gives the basic steps and considerations to prepare for a Healing Conversation. When listeners prepare they are more at ease and better able to ensure the comfort of the elder or dying loved one.

Chapter 11 DEALING WITH UNEXPECTED AND DIFFICULT CIRCUMSTANCES lists the major kinds of surprises listeners are likely to face. It also presents detailed descriptions of behaviors that will help turn those awkward moments into successful interactions.

Section 2 will help you better understand the "how" and "why" Healing Conversations work. Some will read Section 1 and jump in to a Healing Conversation before reading Section 2. You may come back to Section 2 if you run into situations that are challenging and you need guidance. We suggest that you read through these chapters before starting conversations, they will better prepare you to interact with ease and comfort.

HEALING CONVERSATIONS: FROM GETTING TO KNOW THEM BETTER TO LOVING THEM GOODBYE

In this section we share stories of Healing Conversations, which address several important areas of focus: getting to know the elder or dying one better, enhancing or mending relationships, finding peace and acceptance, creative and positive aging, and dealing with serious illnesses and dying. We also tell the stories of the authors' first life-changing Healing Conversations, the experiences that motivated us to write this book.

At the end of each chapter we offer conversation starters and questions you can use to engage in your own Healing Conversations. These sample questions provide a basic format to guide and shape the conversations in a positive way. You may also go to www.HealingConversationsNow.com for more questions. Of course we encourage you to create your own energizing questions based on your curiosity and hopes for your relationship. Email the questions you have used to info@HealingConversationsNow.com, and we will add them to the website, so others can benefit from your experience.

Chapter 1

STORY OF HEALING CONVERSATIONS

INTRODUCTION: THE AUTHORS' FIRST HEALING CONVERSATIONS

It was only long after these initial conversations that we recognized the form, importance and implications of pivotal interactions we each had with parents. Reflecting on those conversations opened our eyes to possibilities for enriched relationships with our elders. When we acted on these opportunities, we were gratified and so were our loved ones. Our first healing conversations follow:

Joan's "Pee" Story

My father was a man of few words, seldom verbalized his thoughts or feelings. I do remember conversations around the kitchen table every night of my growing-up years. He listened mostly. Yet he affirmed his support of me. "We'll make sure you go to whatever college you want and are able to be what you want," he stated one night, even though we were a family of very modest means. However, he and I were not particularly close until he faced death. The crisis helped me dig deep to dredge up enough courage so that I could intervene.

He had been hospitalized for over a month before there was finally a diagnosis: ulcerated colitis. The verdict: his surgeon knew she could fix his body, but that wasn't sufficient. His life force was so weak that she believed his will-to-live would be the deciding factor in the surgery's outcome. Unless he made an affirmative life decision, she wouldn't perform the necessary life-saving operation.

Knowing the surgeon's assessment of the situation, I committed to engaging Dad in a life-defining conversation. I would have to do the talking because of his weakened condition. He would have to make the decision.

My psychologist partner and I constructed a metaphorical story based upon Dad's passion for his work, road construction. In the story we reviewed his accomplishments and challenges and what he loved about life. The story spoke of smooth and rough roads, obstacles in the way, and, most importantly, crossroads. At these places, we can't go straight ahead but have to make crucial decisions about which direction to choose.

I memorized the story by repeating it over and over on my nine-hour drive to visit him.

I was so anxious when I entered his hospital room that I didn't notice the surroundings. Dad was propped up with his eyes closed. I stood at the foot of his bed and started the prepared story – in the telling I left lots of silent space for him to fill in the blanks. The questions were implied. I painted pictures of the precision of his work and the beauty of those roads he'd built through nature. Deep breaths between paragraphs were supposed to help me relax. They didn't.

After I had talked for a few minutes, Dad opened his eyes and asked for a nurse. It was only then that I realized he was holding a urinal under the sheets. I went out of the room shaking. "I messed up. I can't do this! I won't continue." I felt embarrassed at my feeble attempt to save his life by telling him a story. What was I thinking?

When the nurse told me I could return, I was very quiet and determined to stop my useless storytelling. Dad opened his eyes and said, "Will you keep talking to me like that? It is the most relaxed I've felt in a long time. I was finally able to pee."

What a relief! I continued the story; focusing on times he'd made decisions, especially at crossroads. The story metaphorically asked him to make a choice between living and dying. It was Dad's choice, and he chose to live. It was only later that I realized how linked questions, storytelling, and healing can be.

Seventeen years after that crisis he was diagnosed with terminal cancer and given a year to live. We engaged in another round of Healing Conversations. A particularly poignant memory is a conversation around the breakfast table seven months into that last year. He looked up at me, eyes misty, and said, "I'm glad we've had this time. It is good to talk together." Those few words and misty eyes meant so much coming from him. My heart overflowed with gratitude for him and this experience. A few months later, he easily and peacefully took his last breath as Mom and I held his hands.

The power of story was so evident in my relationship with Dad. In this early conversation, I told the story because he was only semiconscious. The question was implied and yet it was powerful: You are at a crossroad; do you choose to live?

Even though I had the life and death interaction with my father years before he was dying, I didn't translate the power of these conversations to more ordinary circumstances until my parents were dying. We missed so much. Realizing lost opportunity makes me sad.

———◆———

Tony also had early and powerful conversations with his parents. Yet, it was not until his mom was dying that the potential of these experiences began to take shape.

Tony: Learning the Whole Story Shifts Everything

It's only in retrospect that I identified my first Healing

Conversation. I thought my learning was going to be about my grandmother, "Granny." Little did I know my biggest learning had to do with my relationship with my dad.

My Granny came to live with us after my grandfather died, when I was in sixth grade. She was often cranky and tough on us kids growing up. I was in my early years of college when Granny died. When I returned home, Dad and I sat looking through a box of her mementos and photos. I took the opportunity to ask him, "What was it like growing up with Granny?"

He shared many stories through photos of his childhood, the trips he went on with his mom and aunt, and the many headaches he gave my grandmother. He told me that when my grandfather died, her life changed drastically. He pointed to a four-foot portrait of her in "the good ole days." In it she reclined on an opulent couch surrounded by her poodles. As a wife, she had lived a very social and active life. When her husband died, that life ended. She had to leave her home and move in with us. She left her friends and all she knew and enjoyed.

Each photo and story gave me a better understanding of her previous life and what she had lost with her husband's premature death. This conversation put her behavior in perspective and allowed me to be more compassionate.

I was grateful to understand my grandmother's life better, but the best part of that conversation was the more satisfying interaction with my dad. I had always felt that he favored my twin brother, the champion athlete. He attended Aaron's wrestling matches and his track meets.

They talked sports. Our conversations to that point had been pretty superficial – "How are things going? -or the conversation focused on Dad.

Mom was the one who usually came to my soccer games, Honor Society ceremonies, and other events. It didn't seem to matter to Dad that I was salutatorian of my class; he was more interested in sports. We just didn't have much of a relationship until that conversation about Granny. Asking about his mother and listening to his stories created more of a bond than we'd ever had. After that conversation, Dad began to ask more about my life and seemed interested and much more engaged with me.

⸺◆⸺

These early conversations are the basis for what we came to define as Healing Conversations. They were so powerful and made such an impression on us we wanted to explore further. We discovered their power to enhance relationships and the quality of interaction among people.

WHY INITIATE HEALING CONVERSATIONS?

Healing Conversations weave a web of connections, a foundation on which to build or rebuild relationships. Inviting our elders to engage in an exploration of their lives through stories, ones that are important to them, begins a process. Being present as we listen to them telling those stores, shifts family dynamics.

Some people enter Healing Conversations primarily because they want to know their loved ones better; they want to create a legacy while the loved one is still capable. Others initiate these conversations with the clear purpose of enhancing or mending relationships. Some hope to find peace and acceptance for themselves and their loved ones. This purpose is likely to be paramount at end-of-life, in that period when people are trying to make sense of their lives and worth. Others hope to age creatively and positively. No matter the reason for initiating them, much can be learned through these intergenerational conversations.

Healing Conversations promise other benefits. The wisdom people garner during a lifetime can teach and guide younger generations. As Louise, a retired teacher, world traveler, and active eighty-four year old said, "I wonder why no one asks me questions." She continued, "It is as if I have nothing to contribute." When we ask elders to share their life experiences, we gain insight and wisdom that may guide and improve our lives. In addition, we show respect for what they've learned and acknowledge elders' ability to contribute.

While writing this book, a different reason for engaging in Healing Conversations became crystal clear. The following story illustrates that point.

Joan's Story:
Laying Foundations for Life Defining Conversations

My phone rang one Saturday night. I was surprised to see my aunt's ID on the screen since she seldom calls me. I usually call her. When I asked how she was she said, " I don't feel very good. I need to talk, and you're the only one I can talk to about this."

She proceeded to tell me that she'd had a call from her doctor's office on Friday. The receptionist told her the doctor wanted her to come in on Monday to talk about the results of a test she'd had. Usually the doctor called directly with results. When the receptionist called, Eva assumed the news was bad. She'd been in pain for a while and feared the worst.

I gave a prayer of appreciation for our years of Healing Conversations. We have talked often of death, dying, and afterlife. By doing so, we'd laid a foundation for this conversation. Her desire and willingness to talk to me had nothing to do with who I am. She could reach out because we had talked about these almost taboo subjects frequently. She had had an opportunity to explore some of her thoughts by voicing them to a non-judgmental person. She knew I would listen without trying to minimize her feelings or change her mind. We'd had conversations about death and dying and were comfortable with each other.

When Eva gets the news on Monday it may or may not be of the catastrophic nature she suspects. It doesn't matter. She is scared and facing the time when she does get the serious diagnosis that announces death is coming soon. I am so grateful that we're able to talk about mortality.

Our spiritual beliefs are incredibly different as are our religious practices. We have little in common on these topics. Yet, we have been able to talk about the life and death issues because we'd had many conversations about fear, death, and dying. When she got scared it was a blessing to both of us that the topic wasn't new. This level of intimate conversation would not have been possible without the years we'd invested together in Healing Conversations.

If we have discussions about death, dying, and the afterlife while our loved ones are still healthy, the topic is theoretical. Then, at critical life junctures it is easier to have the more practical and relevant conversations. They are based on the foundation of previous discussions about death and dying. Joan's Aunt Eva taught her this lesson.

Chapter 2

GIFTS OF KNOWING OTHERS BETTER

Imagine people as wrapped gifts; there is more than meets the eye. Sometimes the wrapping is beautiful. Other times it is worn or put together with little care, yet that doesn't diminish the value of what is inside. What is beneath those outer, more visible layers? Asking questions reveals the person beyond appearances and provides greater connection than the usual ways we know them.

We may have known a person all of our lives but only relate to one aspect of them. Maybe we see them as mom, dad, sister, brother, or friend. What is beyond the usual roles? When we are curious about the multiple aspects of this person, and when we ask questions, we are likely to be surprised. When we invite the whole person into conversation, relationships shift. The person, beyond appearances and usual roles, is likely to come forward. We are many-faceted beings.

When we create an opportunity for people to feel safe, and when we show an interest in them, people will reveal surprising aspects of themselves. As we appreciate what the storyteller shares, trust grows. These conversations allow us to know our elders as whole people and discover the breadth of their experience and wisdom. Knowing them in this way builds understanding and relationship.

What are the rewards for knowing them better?

(1) We understand our heritage and ourselves in new ways, as we know our loved ones better. Their stories create new understanding of our family, heritage, and legacy, which can ripple across generations.

(2) We get to know and appreciate the whole person. As we come to know the other person better, our perception of them expands beyond their usual role in life. We discover more connections and points of interest between us. We also have a backdrop for knowing ourselves better.

Below we explore each of these rewards through the stories of people who discovered them.

UNDERSTAND AND KNOW OUR HERITAGE AND OURSELVES BETTER

As we know elders better, we discover more of ourselves. We might see contrasts or similarities and recognize how those aspects also define our behavior. As we identify themes and patterns of their behavior, we begin to notice how they influence us. We see patterns we want to emulate and some we choose to avoid. These relationships educate us about our own aging and dying. We become familiar with some of the experiences and issues we will face.

In this mobile society most of us no longer grow up with our extended families. Many family members are almost strangers to us. Some live far from family. Others were born after important ancestors were already dead. These conversations give us an understanding of our families of origin and the people in them. We can learn a lot about our ancestors and ourselves by asking the right kind of questions.

Joan's Story: Ancestral Gifts

Eva, my mother's younger sister, had been my role model since I was a little girl. She radiated a light that attracted people to her. She traveled the world, went to museums, the opera, and Broadway plays, and she "dressed to the nines" as my mother would say. When I was a child, her world was one I could only imagine. It seemed exotic.

Yet this worldly woman was also known for her cooking. A meal at her house was a real treat. There were many summer nights that I sat sweating while relishing bowl after bowl of Eva's hot, homemade chicken soup.

This aunt had a distinct energy about her. People noticed her when she walked into a room. I wanted to be just like her.

As an adult, I knew her only as the woman I admired. I didn't know her in a more personal way outside of role model. After my parents died, I decided it was time to be reacquainted with her and could do so by gathering data for her birthday tribute book. I asked her many questions about our family and her life.

The questions and storytelling have continued for thirteen years at this writing. I planned the first conversations with Eva. Some of the questions were: Tell me what you valued most about each of your parents? What early experiences have contributed most to who you are today? Would you paint a picture of each of your parents?

The layers of relationship and appreciation of each other and our heritage grew through these conversations. My frequent visits gave us time to explore. We'd sit at the table and talk over a meal – often in our nightclothes at breakfast. Something about the informality of that setting encouraged sharing. The project began with my desire to know her so I could write a tribute book; surprisingly, it continued and benefited us both. Eva became a whole person beyond a role model. We grew close and I learned a lot about myself too.

Eva's stories also gave me a relationship with grandparents. My grandmother died before I was born, and my grandfather and I had few conversations. He died when I was twelve. Her stories created images and scenes of a life I could begin to imagine as I listened to her. She often talked about how sweet her growing-up years were. Some of her favorite memories centered on being in the kitchen with her mother. No wonder she became such a noted cook.

"I learned by watching my mother," Eva said. "At holidays she made wonderful braided breads. I was so little my eyes just barely came to the top of the table. I'd watch her bake huge loaves of sweet breads and coffee cakes."

Many of Eva's memories of her mother centered around her cooking, baking, walking to farmers' markets for fresh food, and housekeeping. As she relived those treasured times, Eva's eyes got a dreamy look as she transported herself back to those times. It sounded like a lot of work to me, and I said so. Eva replied, " Mom would never call it work. She was a 'balibusta,' a real homemaker. She did every thing with love."

On a different note, as I listened to the stories it became clear that fear was an issue with our family. Eva's Mother always said, "Don't ever take candy or anything from a stranger. If they offer it, run home as fast as you can." Eva said that her mother made an impression.

"I wouldn't even accept candy from a friend's mother, I was so afraid – although I never knew what I was supposed to be scared of," Eva said. That story is one of many accounts that demonstrate my grandmother's apprehension.

Yet when Eva's mother, Fannie, was fourteen, she made

the journey from Europe to the land of opportunity by ship. Alone. Once here, she joined her twin brother, who'd made the trip a year earlier. Together they worked and saved and brought their entire family to this country. What a gargantuan feat for anyone, but particularly for a young girl with so much fear.

That juxtaposition of fear and courage is powerful. The image of fourteen-year-old Fannie, my fearful grandmother, crossing the ocean alone spurs me to action. I remind myself, "If she could do that, I can do anything."

It is such a gift to now have a vivid image of the grandmother I never met. It is grounding to have a sense of this woman; we share a bloodline; she is my ancestor. I recognize in myself many traits Eva described in her mother. Healing Conversations gave me a connection to an ancestor I didn't know. These stories made my grandmother and aunt real for me.

Life stories build bridges between generations. Asking questions begins the process. Lynn opened a doorway of appreciation and legacy by asking his grandfather questions. His desire to know his grandfather was a gift for several generations.

Lynn's Story: Ripples Through the Generations

Thoughts about my grandfather and his life filled my mind in the fall of 1984. He was in good health and seemed content with his life. I was curious about him and

asked Grandpa if I could interview him about his life.
I set up my tape recorder. It worried me when he said,
"Well, I really don't recall much about my life." Then he
described his first day at first grade, the boys he met and
became friends with, his impressions of his first grade
teacher. Then I knew this interview would be a treasure.
For the next hour and a half, he told me stories of his life
as a young boy growing up on a Western farm. He
described how excited he was to go to a boarding school
for eighth grade. It was a chance for real higher educa-
tion. He told how interested he was in algebra and how
much he liked discovering answers to unknowns. He
thought his life was rather unimportant, but I found it full
of triumph and tragedy, and full of vigor.

When I got home from the interview, my father was there
with a couple of bushels of apricots he'd picked from our
trees. Together we stood at the kitchen sink bottling
them. I turned on the tape I had just made, and we listened. Toward the end of the tape, Dad dried his hands
and walked over to the phone. Dialing my uncle, he said,
"Sheldon, you ought to come down and listen to this tape
Lynn just made of Dad. There are things on here I have
never heard before."

Not long after the interview, Grandpa died of cancer. I
am particularly pleased to have the tape. I think Grandpa
would be pleased, too.

Years later, our family was going on vacation, and I put the
tape in the car's player. My children groaned, saying they
didn't want to listen, but I asked them to give it a bit of
time. Once the tape started they listened with rapt attention.

When we came to the part of the story about Grandpa freezing his hands doing the chores he had to do to pay for the boarding school, the children were in awe. Eyes were moist when they heard that Grandpa's father's death meant the end of his schooling. After the tape ended, it was silent in the car for many miles as my sons and my daughter reflected on their great-grandfather's life. My children's thoughtful, silent reaction said their great-grandfather's life was worthy of their reverence.

They know who they are, perhaps partly because in our family there is a tradition of telling family stories. We know who we are through the family stories we share. We cherish Grandfather's tape and its family stories. It is particularly special because it is in his voice.

Lynn's desire to know his grandfather better resulted in a legacy for future generations. Asking him about his life and recording his answers made a difference for Lynn, his father, his uncle, his children, and probably generations to come. Ancestors come to life when future generations hear them speak in their own voices.

With today's technology we can preserve our elders' voices and faces for future generations. Hearing and seeing elders share life stories connects generations. It is a blessing to know and connect with our ancestors and our heritage in this way.

KNOWING AND APPRECIATING
THE WHOLE PERSON

As we learn more about another, our perceptions and understanding change. It is like the old-fashioned film development process. In the darkroom, the developing agent washes over the film. Slowly, a faint image appears, and, in time, it becomes more distinct until a very clear one appears.

When people trust us enough to share their life experiences through stories, we come to know them in an entirely different way. As we see the breadth of their experience, understand what is important to them, and recognize strengths, we gain a fuller understanding of the whole person. We come to appreciate their wisdom and what we can learn from them. When we recognize the context of their decisions and behavior, we may realize we have to let go of old and incomplete stories about them if we are to incorporate our new knowledge of them.

Tony's Story: First Intentional Healing Conversation

My mother was diagnosed with small-cell lung cancer in 2001, and we made that journey together for the next four years. As Mom's hospitalizations became more frequent, something inside nagged at me. I got the message, "It's time to engage in conversations with Mom now."

The conversations I wanted to have with my mother were more personal and difficult than the usual ones. This was not a time to relate superficially. I wanted to hear my mother's life story: her adventures, high points, what she valued most in life. I wanted to know her hopes for the future (for herself, her kids, and her grandkids). I began jotting down questions that would help us connect, and that would help me to understand her better. I realized that I needed support.

I reached out to professional colleagues who interview for a living. These people specialize in asking appreciative and energizing questions. I wanted to know what questions they would ask of their mother, father, sister, brother, husband, wife, or loved one as end of life neared. I received a flood of positive support, over 100 responses. We share some of those responses in this book.

They helped me form questions that were different from those I'd thought of before. I chose a number of them to ask my mother, and her responses and stories fascinated me. One of the first things I asked was, "Tell me a story about your life before you were married."

Her answer was instantaneous, and her eyes sparkled as she said, "Travel. As soon as Betty Lou, my best friend, and I graduated from high school, we packed up and left Kentucky; we moved to Florida. I loved to travel and hoped for many adventures."

I knew that she had married early and was a mother by age twenty. Her big travel dreams must have collided with reality. She had five children by the time she was twenty-seven. Traveling was quite limited. I wondered if my own travel bug came from her.

My mother responded positively to the questions. Her responses and stories captivated me; even more important, our conversations created a much deeper connection between us. She explored key life choices, decisions, and even regrets – helping me to truly understand my mom's life and decisions more fully. Although I had known her all my life, she shared things I had never heard before.

I'm honored to have journeyed with my mom: knowing that each and every part of her life has had an impact on my life and choices. Her stories helped me piece together the mystery of her life and to understand my own better. I'm forever grateful and forever changed.

Reflecting on my experience with Mom, I'm glad I had some sense of urgency and began the conversations when I did. Mom had sudden onset of dementia and died soon after quite unexpectedly. Her death certainly jolted me. "Now" is the time to ask questions and get to know our loved ones better. We don't know what next week or next month will bring.

The following story illustrates how investing time getting to know your loved one may change the relationship dramatically for you – and possibly for the elder.

Pam's Story: Real Father Discovered

We had a crazy childhood: My father and mother were both alcoholics. I called them Charlie and Sally. Denial was the approach of choice in our alcoholic family. If anyone dared to mention the elephant in the living room, everyone conspired to deny its existence. It meant that honest communication at an emotional level was rare. The craziness continued as my parents aged. For six years, I stayed away from them. It was just too difficult to see their lives or interact with them.

Just before my mother was given a terminal diagnosis, Dad had gone to a dry-out place. He wasn't drinking as actively during my mother's illness, and our relationship shifted. We both recognized that time is not infinite, and we needed to make the best of what was available to us. We started spending more time together.

After Mom's death, I took my dad to Normandy, France. I knew he'd been there on D-Day, and the fiftieth anniversary was approaching. I prepared for the trip by reading about D-Day and learned how horrific that day had been. Going there with Dad was truly moving.

There's a place in Normandy called Point du Hoc where we saw deep pits in the earth where bombs had exploded. Charlie walked by a hole and noted, "A ninety-millimeter bomb made that one." He was acutely aware and still had the skill set to identify what caliber of bomb had made each hole.

While we were there, he told me that he was twenty-three and the oldest in his battalion on D-Day. He saw his fellow GIs blown up in front of him. Blood and bodies were all over the place. As I listened, tears of gratitude for what he'd endured rolled down my cheeks.

I began to imagine what it must have been like for a young soldier to live through that horror. Seeing his reaction to the acre upon acre of crosses, I started to understand the profound impact that experience had on him. It shifted his life and put a pall over it.

As I knew more about his life, I began to understand the complexity of it and to recognize what he had gone through. I came to believe that those events were the reason for his alcoholism. Living through that war experience, then coming back to Pleasantville, USA, was crazy. You can't go from the death and the destruction of war to an idyllic life in the United States and still be sane. My understanding of what he'd been through deepened, and I appreciated him more. Our relationship shifted again.

In 1998, six months after we returned from our third trip to Europe, I went to North Carolina to celebrate my father's birthday. I got there and realized that he hadn't unpacked from our trip yet. He said he couldn't find certain things and thought someone had stolen them. When I unpacked his bag, I found his dirty clothes and those things he thought were missing. I realized this was a clear indication of his memory loss. A year later he moved into an assisted living facility near me in Maine. Wednesday became Charlie's night. I was careful to set boundaries, so I didn't get burned out. If I did, there was no one else to be with him. I told him I'd see him once a week. Wednesday night became sacred time. He could count on it.

I'd arrive in time to have dinner with him in the dining room, and then we'd go up to his small apartment. Dad had the TV on twenty-four hours a day, so we'd sit and watch it together, interspersed with conversation. Sometimes scenes or dialogue on TV sparked his memory, and he'd tell stories. One of his favorite stories was about a time when my sister was a toddler. He was zipping up her coat and caught her chin. She cried. He felt so bad because he'd hurt her, that he cried too. Every visit, I learned something else about him, and these conversations continued to shift the relationship.

On one of my Wednesday visits, Charlie exclaimed that he'd never hit us girls. I replied, "Yes, you did. One Saturday morning after you'd worked late and wanted to sleep. We were making noise. You picked up a hairbrush and hit me several times on my bottom."

Instead of denying my reality as he'd done all of my life, he said, "I'm sorry."

I felt validated in the deepest sense of the word, hearing this from him. He didn't deny my memory or story. It was accepted, and I felt heard. That was rare. Our family had operated on denial. It was like, finally, a sense of relief. Through these conversations and experiences, I started to see my father in a different light. I saw more depth than I'd previously recognized in him. For so many years, I had only seen him as a drunk and a burden. By spending time together and knowing him better, I got to have a father – a different one.

Pam invested time and energy in a new relationship with her father. One that was caring and open. She allowed her understanding of him to shift and began to acknowledge and celebrate how he had changed. By doing so, she gained a sense of connection to her father.

Knowing another person more fully can make the difference between appreciating and judging. It is easy to criticize and take offense when we focus on a snippet of behavior or conversation. As conversation partners share, we engage, connect, and appreciate each other more. As we understand our loved ones in a broader context, relationships shift.

The stories above highlight ways of getting to know our loved ones better, from understanding the whole person to creating a legacy. Taking the time to engage with our elders and dying loved ones is essential if we want understanding and love. These conversations form the foundation for enhancing and mending relationships, which we explore more deeply in the next chapter.

QUESTIONS AND CONVERSATION STARTERS FOR KNOWING THEM BETTER

In this section, we give you some questions to use as conversation starters. There are more available on line at www.HealingConversationsNow.com. We encourage you to share questions you have asked and the kinds of responses on our website. As they are posted, we will develop a community question board.

The questions below range from general to more specific. The broader ones are open questions, which allow storytellers to scan their entire life experience and decide what story they want to share. Other questions are more specific and focus on a particular topic: such as childhood friends and values you live by.

The questions that follow are the heart of Healing Conversations. They ask about exceptional moments, strengths, and other key aspects of the storyteller's life. They are designed to get to know the essence and core that define the storyteller.

Understand and Know our
Heritage and Ourselves Better

High point: In each of our lives certain times stand out as exceptional, some people call them peak experiences. During these times we feel alive, engaged, and energized. Please tell a story about a time that stands out as a high point for you.

Follow-up:
- What were you doing?
- Who were you with?
- What makes this situation special to you?
- What about that time has made a difference and what is it?

Family History and Heritage: Would you share a story that illustrates the things that are most important to know about our family before I was born? It might describe people, events, values or traditions that had an impact on our family in some way.

Follow-up:
- What was it like for you growing up in our family?
- What are some positive memories, key events, and milestones that stand out for you?
- What made/makes our family unique?
- What do you consider the strengths of our family?

Your Family: Family is central in our lives, as are the unique relationships with each family member. Please tell me a memorable story about your relationship with a family member (parent, sibling, child, grandparent, close relative) that shaped who you are.

Follow-up:
- What happened and who was involved?
- What effect did this person have on you?
- How has this person contributed to your life?

Childhood friend: Please share a story about a childhood friend who made a difference in your life. Talk about this friendship and the person.

Follow-up:
- How did you meet?
- What did you like to do together?
- What positive impact did this person have on your life?
- What was/is most rewarding about this friendship?

Your Spouse/Life Partner: One of the most important relationships is the one with a spouse/life partner – the person you have chosen to adventure with through life in good times and bad. Please share a story that demonstrates some of the things that stand out most about your spouse/life partner.

Follow-up:
- What are the unique qualities, strengths, and values that made you choose this person as a spouse/life partner?
- How did you know this was a person you wanted to make a commitment to?

- How has this relationship brought joy, contentment, and pleasure to your life?

Knowing and Appreciating the Whole Person

Accomplishments: Without being humble, talk about
some of the accomplishments you are most proud of. We
each achieve more than we may recognize, so be sure to
consider examples that might not seem all that extraordinary to you. Think about comments others have made
that recognized your accomplishments.
Follow-up:
- How did you achieve these accomplishments?
- Who and what supported your success?
- What do you value most about these accomplishments?
- What long-term effect have these accomplishments had on your life?

Important People in Your Life: Please tell a story of an
important person in your life (friend, loved one, col-
league, etc.), one who made a big difference. You might
have known him or her for a short time or for a lifetime,
yet that person had a lasting and positive impact on you.
Follow-up:
- What is it about this person that you value
  most?
- How has this person made your life better?
- What was necessary to maintain this friendship?

Role of Work in Your Life: Everyone works at either paid jobs, unpaid by necessity or in a volunteer capacity. In many ways, the work we choose is an opportunity to express the best of who we are. Please share a story that illustrates the importance of the work you chose.
Follow-up:
• What first attracted you to this work?
• Please highlight how your passion for this work has shaped you as a person?
• What do/did you value most about your work and profession?
• What rewards and benefits have you gained from working?

Values You Live By: Even if we don't talk about them directly, most of us have values that guide our decisions and actions. We may think of them as the rules we live by. What values are important to you?
Follow-up:
• How have these values positively impacted your life and relationships?
• Please share a story about how one of your core values influenced your behavior and actions?

Turning Points: Would you tell a story about a turning point in your life, a time that changed your direction?
Follow-up:
• What happened and who was involved?
• What decisions did you make and how did you make them?
• How did your life change because of this turning point?
• What did you learn from this experience?

Chapter 3

ENHANCE AND MEND RELATIONSHIPS

This chapter focuses on intergenerational relationships. We might love a dear one and yet only know her or him in certain roles. We may feel close to someone and yet not share the degree of intimacy that would be most satisfying. In these cases, Healing Conversations will enhance the connection.

You may have other relationships that have become difficult or strained. Whether you see these people regularly or not there is an emotional distance between you. In these situations, we suggest several approaches to mending the relationship.

ENHANCE RELATIONSHIPS

In the process of getting to know your conversation partner better, the bonds between you will strengthen and broaden. You may find more unexpected commonalities. You may understand your loved one in a way that makes you feel closer. Below is Joan's (author's) story of her relationship with her beloved aunt, Eva. After Joan's parents died her relationship with her aunt shifted as they spent many hours in conversation over a number of years.

Joan's story:
Distant Admiration Turns into Intimate Caring

Alone. There is only one relative between me and the role of being the oldest. I am the next one to die. Some would call me an orphan since both parents had died. I'd read about aging and facing this phenomenon of being the one on the front line, when there is no older generation between death and me. Now I was experiencing it. All of my parent's siblings were long gone – except Eva, my mother's younger sister.

I'd always admired Eva. She was my childhood role model even though she and my mother had a frosty relationship. When I grew up, married, and moved to Maine from Delaware there were gaps of time when we didn't see each other. We were less connected than during my childhood.

In my mind, Eva remained the sophisticated, attractive, and fun single aunt I'd always admired, but we weren't close. She wasn't the one I'd call to talk with about life. She was a fascinating woman at a distance – literally and figuratively.

However, one day, when I was pondering my orphan situation, I called her. "Now that Mom and Dad are gone, you are my only relative. You are as close to a mother as I have."

Silence.

I'd called her out-of-the-blue, and she wasn't prepared for my almost pleading invitation. Besides, it isn't exactly a compliment to say, "you're it by default." I didn't know exactly what I wanted and had dropped, unexpectedly, into the conversation. Eva could not possibly have been prepared for this request.

I didn't give up. Instead, I took the opportunity to know her better. Her eightieth birthday was approaching, and I decided to create a tribute book so Eva could know how much she meant to me – even if we hadn't had much contact in decades.

So began the ritual of visiting Eva and Nettie, the only remaining sibling of the family that brought Eva into their fold when she no longer had parents. They had lived together for more than forty years. They welcomed my visits. We'd sit around the table talking for hours.

At first I gathered family history, so I could write the tribute book. Those conversations continued for years after the book was complete – they go on today. They were Healing Conversations. At first they allowed me to know Eva and my family better. Yet, as these intimate and appreciative conversations do, they brought us closer.

Nettie died at ninety-five a couple of years ago. Eva is in

her nineties. Our phone calls are sweet. Our visits, every six-weeks, are relaxing and fulfilling. Over the years, we slowly talked about the issues between my mother and Eva. We opened our hearts to each other. One day in the last two years she said, "You know, Kiddo, I didn't completely accept you at first."

"I know," I said. Smiling inside because obviously she would never have said this if that situation hadn't reversed itself. I am so glad we engaged in these conversations, they helped us to discover and love each other in a much fuller way.

At first, she was my role model at a distance. Now we have a loving relationship that connects us intimately. We both live alone and at a distance except we have each other. She knows I will drop everything and be there if there is an emergency. I know I can call her, breathe, relax, and enjoy our connection. We look forward to laughing with each other. I am grateful for the conversations and her willingness to participate. They were the bridge that gave us a "real" connection.

The story above highlights how relationships can be enhanced through persistence, intention, and time invested. Even when you think you have a wonderful relationship, it is likely it will be enhanced as you get to know your loved one in a more whole way. Listening in a connected way adds a measure of closeness and caring.

MEND RELATIONSHIPS

Many of us do not have the relationship we would most like to have with certain family members or dear friends. Often when loved ones do an inventory of unresolved issues, conflicts and rifts top the list. As people review their lives, old dysfunctional patterns of relating may be the norm, though painful and hurtful. The conflict may be generations old and its origin forgotten. In the present time, what is most salient is the desire to move beyond those things that put distance between the conversation partners.

The nature of the rift will guide the types of conversations you have and the questions you ask. Deep seated conflicts may require building trust over time, before addressing the conflict directly. You may want to involve the loved one in "getting to know you" kinds of conversations and questions as outlined in the previous chapter. For less ingrained conflicts, you may be able to engage directly in the types of conversations and questions suggested below.

We propose four possible approaches to mend relationships: 1) building a bridge of trust by getting to know the other better, 2) acknowledging multiple perspectives and versions of any story, 3) changing your actions to change the dynamics, and 4) reframing the situation. Sometimes it takes a third party to facilitate mending difficult relationships. We address each of these approaches in this chapter.

Building a Bridge of Trust

When the relationship is troubled, it is hard to connect meaningfully. People keep a guarded distance. Beliefs and behaviors are habituated in a way that reinforces separation. People are hypersensitive and on the lookout for problems. If the relationship is to change, it is helpful to identify incorrect assumptions and be open to exploring new perceptions. It is encouraging to remember that a slight shift in perception or behavior has a significant impact and can make a huge difference. Preparation and willingness are keys to successful resolution of conflicts.

A number of stories in chapter two illustrate building bridges and trust. Tony, Pam, and Joan share stories that illustrate what can happen to relationships when we take time to get to know our loved ones. Both people benefit and are enriched. Healing Conversations, which invite conversation partners to know each other more fully, build bridges that invite trust and connection.

Acknowledging Multiple Perspectives

We have designed an activity that is helpful in acknowledging different perspectives of a single situation. It is "The Whole

Story" activity. It invites each participant to reflect on his or her own story, recognize it as incomplete, and acknowledge there is more than one valid version of the story or situation.

It can be done alone or with the people involved in a conflict. If there is enough trust, those involved in the conflict might do this exercise together. If there is quite a bit of distance between you or resistance in either conversation partner, prepare by doing the exercise yourself, before involving the elder or dying loved one.

"The Whole Story" activity invites participants to step out of their habitual way of thinking about a situation and/or person, so they are able to see it anew. It invites them to expand their thinking and open their minds to new ways of perceiving the situation or person. It shines light on the fact that there is more than one version of any story. No one of us has the whole truth. Hearing – or even imaging the other's version of the event – opens our minds to expanded ways of understanding.

The Whole Story: When there has been a rift, we usually have a story about it, one that justifies and explains why we are so hurt, angry, or frustrated. We have probably told it many times. Each time we tell it our version becomes more real to us; we believe it must be true. The key to unlocking many conflicts is to get outside of our own perceptions, what we believe is the "true" story, and recognize that others have very different perceptions of the situation. They have their own and different story. As we understand their version of the story, our stance may soften and our need for distance may diminish.

Step 1: Remember the story as you've told it in the past. As you bring it to mind, notice how you feel as you think about that story and the people involved. Do any parts of you get tense? Does your voice change if you are speaking?

Step 2: Retell the story from a different point of view. Imagine you are any of the characters in your story except yourself. In your mind's eye, see the event or behavioral pattern from the other's frame of reference, and tell what you imagine is that person's story.

Stretch your mind to think of possibilities you haven't considered before. Be generous as you imagine their motives, beliefs, past experiences, and assumptions about you, the relationship, and the situation. See how thoroughly you can step into their shoes so that the situation looks different. How might they see or hear it differently from you? Be creative, generous, and courageous.

Step 3: Reflect on what was different when you spoke from another's point-of-view. What is different when you tell the story from the other's frame of reference? What are the shifts?

Step 4: Summarize what you discovered. Reflect on the "The Whole Story" inquiry. What thoughts and feelings stirred within you? What surprised you most? What do you see or understand differently now that you have done the preparation? What might you do differently in this Healing Conversation?

This activity is designed to highlight the many possible perspectives and versions brought to any story or situation. When participants enter into this activity with creativity and a desire to learn, they are often surprised. If they hadn't thought about another perspective, the activity helps them to see more of the whole picture.

Change Your Actions to Change Your Relationship

This approach to mending relationships highlights changing a listener's behavior, even slightly. It is likely the storyteller's behavior will also shift. The next story tells how the listener actively did something different in order to improve a difficult relationship. Being creative in her approach to her mother allowed Mary Lou to have a much easier time when she visited with her.

Mary Lou had always feared her critical and demanding mother. She felt obligated to visit occasionally and dreaded these encounters. Her mother's criticism continued. In addition, her mother had begun repeating the same stories over and over – they had been boring the first time around, and they only got worse. When she got an idea for a different approach and changed her behavior, dynamics shifted.

Mary Lou's story: Questions Are the Answer

I was always afraid of my mother and her judgments: she had her standards. They were so instilled in me she didn't need to speak them. I learned the "right" way early. There was a proper way to dress and sit and comport yourself. (During this interview Mary Lou was 84. She must be five-feet-ten and quite slim. She stands up straight and tall, and looks quite striking in her pressed and creased jeans.)

I was always afraid Mom would blow up. Mom needed to be so good. She had to be nice, help others, and do the right thing. However, the pressure from being so perfect would build up, and she'd blow. I never knew when it would happen, and so I was always apprehensive.

As she aged, none of my siblings wanted her to live with them. I didn't want her to live with me, either. Even visits with her were difficult. We were all relieved when she decided to move to a retirement home in Michigan—far away from us. It was easier.

Even then I dreaded going to visit her. Mom always told the same stories over and over; I was tired of listening to them. My friend Bobbi and I talked about this problem many times — we're both social workers. Bobbi suggested I intervene. Instead of allowing Mom to ramble through her stories, I could take charge by initiating positive inquiry and direct the conversation by asking questions about my mother's life. On my next visit, I brought a recorder and started asking Mom questions that interested me. At first Mom said she couldn't participate in that, but I just continued setting up the recorder, and finally she began to loosen up.

Asking questions and taping allowed me to be in control; I wasn't afraid anymore. As I sat and listened to my mother, I heard wonderful, interesting stories. I could ask any question I wanted. These sessions gave me a clearer picture of my mother, of all aspects of her character and personality — things I had never heard before. At the very least, I became more comfortable with her and noted things we had in common.

Mary Lou shifted her behavior. She came to the visit prepared with questions about topics of interest to her and a determination to make visits better. She became a curious listener and had the comfort of knowing she had some ability to direct the conversation. She didn't confront her mother or talk about their differences.

Changing her behavior was enough to impact the interactions in a positive way. Doing so paved a path between the two. Mary Lou related that at one point after she started recording her mother they were both in the kitchen. Her mom was drying the dishes unusually slowly and deliberately as she talked. It dawned on Mary Lou that this was her mother's way of extending the conversation. Healing Conversations can improve and mend relationships, or at least bring some degree of healing and closure.

⟞⬦⟝

Reframing – Appreciative Listening

Reframing is a tool that helps us see a person or situation from a different frame of reference, a different point-of-view. When we reframe a situation we are able to understand more of the whole. It is like walking around an object and seeing it from all angles. With people, situations, and stories, reframing gives a fuller picture and broader understanding. It allows us to move beyond a habitual way of knowing someone or situation.

One way to reframe is by asking questions that require the person responding to take a different point-of-view, one that helps them to recognize other possible versions of the story or situation. Problems can be reframed by asking people to turn what they define as problems into opportunities.

We can reframe by listening appreciatively, with an open mind ready to understand another from a different frame-of-reference. Doing so, we hear our loved ones differently and can appreciate their point-of-view. Reframing means seeing and hearing the event in a new context, giving a different interpretation of the behavior that might annoy us. Shifting our frame of reference may shift the relationship.

One view is not more correct or right than the other. We can choose to focus on the version that is most likely to build relationship.

Yaeko's Story of Reframing

My mother is 91 and lives alone in an apartment in Japan. She has always been extraordinarily strong-willed and had clear opinions. Many people react negatively to her strong ideas, and some family members are alienated from her because of them. It took me many years to appreciate this characteristic. In fact, we had many heated arguments and disagreements until I had a realization.

One day during an argument something happened to me. I stopped my usual thoughts. All of a sudden I realized: the reason my mom is strong enough to live alone and not ask any of us for help at age 91 is exactly this part of her, her strong will. This characteristic is very positive. After that, I stopped fighting with her. Instead I admired her strength. From then on, I didn't try to change her or resist her so much. It seemed better for both of us.

Yaeko's ability to step back and see her mother through a different lens is an important aspect of reframing. Doing so expands the pool of possible explanations for behavior. When we recognize multiple interpretations, we can choose the one that will add most to the relationship.

Facilitating Other's Healing Conversations

The next story describes Tony's use of Healing Conversations to facilitate some mending of the relationship between his mom and sister, Tanya. He supported their conversation by bringing them together and suggesting possible questions. Then he let go of the outcomes.

Tony recognized his mother's time was limited, and he was concerned about Tanya who was estranged from their mom. They had had a distant relationship for many years and had almost no contact with one another. Tony and his sister had very different experiences and relationships with their mom. When Tony and his twin, Aaron, were born, the two older sisters, Tanya and Stephanie, were sent to live with a friend. That significant decision disrupted the family and had a lasting effect on the girls' relationship with their mother.

Tony's Story:
Make the Most of this Last Opportunity

My sister Stephanie died of cancer when she was 26, over twenty years ago now. During the time she was battling cancer, my twin brother, Aaron, would hardly ever visit. After Stephanie's death, he was distraught and often repeated; "I should have visited her more often. I should have been there for her."

I didn't want Tanya to have the same regrets about our mother that Aaron had about our sister. Knowing there were a number of unresolved issues between them, I called to let Tanya know of Mom's worsening condition and my concerns. After a long conversation, she agreed to fly from Colorado to Connecticut for a visit with Mom and me.

It had helped me to think of questions in preparation for my own Healing Conversations with Mom. So before Tanya came, I put some questions together that might facilitate new and different conversations for them. I e-mailed the questions to Tanya so she could think about them as she prepared for the reunion with Mom. Before the trip Tanya e-mailed me:

"Your questions are all good ones, so thank you for thinking through them. Unfortunately, I think that they are just a bit too late for where I am. To be honest, I am not looking for a renewed connection w/Mom, but I suppose some sort of closure might be a good idea. I know it's not what you want to hear, but it's just how it is. I don't bear a grudge in my heart any longer. But I have moved on thru sheer hard work & determination to survive, and I don't feel good about her or the childhood I did (or didn't) have. I wish I could make it different, but I can't. Who knows how I will feel when I see her, but I don't want her or you to be disappointed."

"I am glad that you have pushed me to come back & see her. Thank you. Again, who knows how I will feel when faced w/seeing her... I just don't know & am quite anxious about talking to her... Looking forward to seeing you. I love you! XOXO Tanya"

I responded to Tanya's e-mail and assured her "As I said, no pressure, just a possible way to find the closure you desire, and maybe some sort of renewed connection. I love you a lot, and we are all looking forward to seeing you."

I picked up Tanya from the airport and drove her to visit our mom. When we got to the rehab unit, it was a bit awkward. Mom hadn't seen Tanya since my wedding two years before, and it had been a number of years before that since they had been in the same room together. So after a hello and a hug of my own, I quickly left Tanya and Mom alone to talk.

Immediately after the visit, Tanya didn't share many details of the conversation or what had happened. However, a few months later, she sent an e-mail that gave me some clues. She indicated the kind of connection she was able to make – and even her ability to identify with Mom.

"Sounds like Mom is getting a bit more ready to let go. I can't believe how hard she has fought. Amazing really, but not surprising. I think I have that piece of her in me, the real fighter — for good & bad. I was also thinking I should call her. Can you send me the number please?"

"Again, I want to thank you for having me come out there in August. It was really good for me & hopefully for her as well. Now I just feel so sad for her & surely wouldn't want my life to end without some closure around my relationships, especially with my children. I can only hope my children will be as supportive for me as you've been for her."

"By the way, I'll send along some pictures and a note for Mom that you can print. I'm sure even if you print them at home she'll be happy."

I was pleased and relieved that Tanya came to visit and wouldn't have the same regrets my brother had after Stephanie died. I was grateful for the understanding and new awareness Tanya gained through the conversations. The results were pretty powerful, considering Tanya probably didn't understand Mom's earlier choices any better afterwards. It seemed that Tanya recognized and found some peace in the fact that Mom may not have been able to, or was unwilling to, revisit certain parts of her past that were just too painful. Tanya walked away from that visit no longer needing to know why Mom did what she did – that was okay.

I know my mom was happy to have reconnected with Tanya. Whenever I phoned or visited, she would ask about Tanya and her family – and would light up when she saw their pictures or when I shared a story about them. It isn't a fairy tale ending. However, I know that brief interaction between my sister and my mother was healing for us all.

While Healing Conversations provide a format for shifting relationships, both parties must have some degree of willingness. Some people are so wounded they may not be able to imagine letting go of the pain. Some are willing to try; others take their burdens to the grave.

—————

Relationships can be improved even if people are unable to fully forgive each other. Family members can encourage others to have Healing Conversations, and can even invite and facilitate them as Tony did. We issue invitations knowing that we aren't in control of others' behavior. The relationship requires two people, and each will contribute or not. Yet even a slight shift brings a greater degree of comfort and a sense of acceptance or peace.

In summary, Healing Conversations address rifts in a different way from many conflict-resolution practices. Healing Conversations are a way to throw a rope across a chasm as an invitation to reach out to each other. They build connections by reminding people of what is important to them in the relationship; as they focus on the benefits of connecting it is easier to be gracious to each other and to find a way to go beyond their differences. Ways of bridging the gap include telling the story of the rift, then retelling the story from another perspective, and reflecting on how that makes a difference, listen. Reframing the situation from another angle is another way of resolving a conflict. It is a process of connecting rather than confronting. It takes courage and persistence and there are no guarantees. However, there is hope. The following questions and conversation starters are a good first step to enhance or mend a relationship with a loved one.

QUESTIONS AND CONVERSATION STARTERS TO ENHANCE AND MEND RELATIONSHIPS

There are two categories of questions in this section: the first focuses directly on enhancing the relationship between the conversation partners, and the second set is designed to mend relationships. The questions and conversation starters in every chapter of section 1 will strengthen relationships.

However, questions in the Enhance Our Relationship section below are different. They focus directly on the relationship between the listener and storyteller. They ask both people to remember the positive elements and what they value most about their connection. Acknowledging these appreciated aspects of the relationship is likely to connect people in a more meaningful way.

Unlike many Healing Conversations, when focusing directly on the relationship, the conversation partners may take turns answering questions. Trade roles as listener and storyteller so that you both have the privilege of hearing and being heard, thoroughly and without interruption. The listener might take the first turn answering the questions below in order to model and demonstrate the willingness to risk speaking about the relationship. People who have shared this experience report becoming much closer during and after the conversation.

Enhance Our Relationship

Many relationships are quite satisfying and yet, it is possible to add value to them by talking directly about them. Exploring the relationship, itself, is a way of expanding and amplifying the connections. The next set of questions is designed to explore what conversation partners value most about each other and the relationship.

Best of Our Relationship: As you look back on our relationship, tell me about a time that stands out as a high point – a meaningful and important story that captures the best of our relationship.
Follow-up:
- What were we doing?
- What stands out as important and essential about our relationship?
- What do you value about that aspect of our relationship?

Respect/Admire: Respect and admiration are essential relationship building blocks – when respect and admiration are there, so is the foundation for a strong relationship. Tell about a time when you felt admired and/or respected in our relationship.
Follow-up:
- What was the situation?
- How did you know you were respected or admired?
- How has that respect/admiration influenced our relationship?

Making the Relationship Even Better: Looking forward in time, imagine our relationship has developed, and it is better than ever. Describe what you see that is new, different, and better.

Follow-up:

- In your enhanced image of us, what are we doing/not doing that adds value to our relationship?
- What is most important to you about the different behavior?
- Imagine the smallest step we took that had the greatest positive impact on our relationship? What was it?

Mend Our Relationship

A rift causes a tear in the fabric of the relationship. You can reweave the web of connections between you, if you acknowledge the importance of the relationship and your desire to rebuild it. Remember to honor small steps and shifts.

Appreciate your own willingness to go beyond the issues that separate you, and invite the other to join you in that endeavor. Hopefully, both of you will come to this conversation with a clear intention to put the relationship first. We start with relationship rebuilding questions; they are designed to create a foundation of trust strong enough so that you can directly address the differences if that still seems useful. The last question is designed for that purpose.

These questions are intended to focus on the strengths and

valued components of the relationship. Doing so reminds people of what they appreciated about the connection and what makes it worthwhile to mend it.

> **Good Times:** Every relationship has its ups and downs. Even the toughest ones have some positive moments. Please think about a positive experience or highpoint of our relationship and talk about it.
> *Follow-up:*
> - What were we doing?
> - What made this experience stand out as important?
> - What do you value most about that experience?

> **Appreciation: a gift to be shared.** Even if it is a stretch, even if you haven't seen these assets for a while, please share three qualities, skills, or things you appreciate most about me and/or our relationship.
> *Follow-up:*
> - Remember times when you recognized those qualities in our interactions or in me. What was I/we doing?
> - What do you value most about those characteristics?

> **Common Ground:** We all view the world in different ways and have different values and beliefs. We live our lives in different ways. Differences can separate, but common ground unites us. What are the important things we have in common? Would you tell a story about a time when these commonalities added to our relationship?

Follow-up:
- What do you value most about these commonalities?
- How can we build on these commonalities to strengthen our relationship?

Acceptance: Each person is unique in how they act, behave, interact, and make decisions. Some we agree with, others we don't. However, acceptance is a key to mending relationships. Tell me about a time when we found loving tolerance and acceptance for each other – even in spite of our unique differences?
Follow-up:
- What were those core factors that enabled this acceptance?
- What would increase our acceptance for each other even more?

Our Different Perceptions: Describe a situation or event that is dividing you. Ask if the other is willing to explore each other's perceptions of that situation as a way to understand each other better and possibly move beyond this conflict. Continue only if the other is genuinely ready and willing, otherwise, agree to disagree. If there is agreement to continue, the initiator might say:

> We see (a situation or person) through very different lens. I want to understand your perceptions and beliefs concerning (the situation or person). I am willing to hear something new and different. Would you tell me how you see the situation or person? (Listener must be silent and practice connected listening rather than respond with his or her perceptions.)

Follow-up:
- Tell me more.
- What matters most to you about this situation (person)?
- What about the situation (or person) are you most curious about?
- What do you wish I'd understand differently?
- What do you want to ask me about my understanding of the situation (person)?

Be careful and attentive to your own reactions during this exercise. You might want to explain yourself, but that will ruin the purpose of this activity. When the first speaker is finished – indicates they are complete in relating their point of view about the event – you might summarize what you heard the other say and ask if you heard correctly. If so you might go on to say, "Listening to you is very helpful. May I share how I experienced the same situation, so that we better understand each other and move beyond our different experiences?

Chapter 4

FINDING PEACE AND ACCEPTANCE

Wise ones remind us that peace in the world begins within each of us. It is an inside out job. No matter our age, it is an accomplishment to find peace and acceptance of self and life. The particular tasks of coming to peace when nearing death are discussed in chapter 7, Loving Them Goodbye. In this chapter we focus on finding peace and acceptance at any age.

We begin this chapter with a story that illustrates the quality of peace and acceptance that is possible. The story is about a mother and daughter who are at peace with each other, death, and life as it is. Then we define two processes leading to peace and acceptance. They are: answering universal questions and completing unfinished business. We end the chapter with questions listeners can ask to encourage elders and dying loved ones to find their own peace and acceptance.

ACHIEVING PEACE AND ACCEPTANCE

Those who work or live with elders and dying people know the remarkable difference between those resisting life as it is, and those who accept their circumstances. The first are suffering and make their situation more difficult. The latter are at peace maybe even as they cope with some form of pain. They are accepting.

Acceptance isn't the same as lethargy; it is not passively taking what comes. Instead, it entails reflecting on life and appreciating the gifts of life, love, and learning. When people are peaceful they are likely present, mindful, and centered. They may have a heightened sense of gratitude. Peace is a sense that all-is-well, no matter the external conditions; peace is an inside job. It comes when people accept and trust that they can deal with whatever life presents.

Achieving a peaceful state can be quite a mysterious process. If listeners can find that place of comfort within themselves, their presence and state of acceptance is likely to be contagious and help the loved one find his or her own sense of peace. One task for listeners, especially when dealing with troubled elders or dying loved ones, is to be as peaceful, calm, and as present as possible. The conversation partner is likely to match their peaceful state, as part of the silent conversation.

It is likely that both people in the next story were at peace with their situation, and their individual acceptance reinforced each other's well-being.

Beth and her elder mother are examples of people who are comfortable and at peace with life-as-it-is.

Beth's Story: A Little Bit of Heaven

I had no plans for taking care of my mother at the end of her life. My life situation just put me in the place to be the only one of four siblings who had the freedom to move in with Mom. She wanted to stay in her own home but couldn't unless someone stayed with her. I said, "I'll just relocate for as long as I can." I ended up staying with her from the time she was 80 until she died at 92.

When I made the decision to stay with her, one of my daughters-in-law said, "It must be difficult to put your life on hold."

It was one of those times when you hear yourself speak without thinking, and know it is the truth. I said, "My life isn't on hold. This is my life." I hadn't planned it this way. Yet I realized that my life was about being with my mom at this special time and allowing her to live these final years in her own home, as she chose to live them.

Mom was a perfect model of aging gracefully and just being happy with the simplest things. She was a joy to be with. For instance, she loved her breakfast. Every morning, she'd come out and say, "I just can't wait for my breakfast. I just love my breakfast."

During the last five years of her life, we vacationed for two or three weeks each summer at a lovely little place on Bailey Island overlooking Harpswell Bay in Maine. She would sit on the deck in the sun and watch the waves break just below us. One day, as she gazed at the ocean, she sighed, "This is a little bit of heaven."

In the summer of 2000, halfway through our three-week vacation, she surprised me. We had a ritual of saying, "Good night. I love you," and going off to bed. That night when she told me she loved me, I replied, "I know that, Mom."

She said, "No, I want you to hear it because I may not be here in the morning to tell you again."

I said, "You'll be here, Mom."

Morning came and she toddled out with her walker, in her fuzzy pink bathrobe. I said, "Good morning, Mom. How are you?"

She responded, "I have a little pain in my tummy. I think I'm really hungry. Can I have an extra-big breakfast?"

She went out on the deck while I made fried eggs, bacon, toast, and coffee. She ate every mouthful of her beloved breakfast. After I'd cleaned up the dishes, I went out and asked Mom about the pain in her tummy. She said, "I still have it, and I feel a little bit dizzy." Half an hour later she was quite dizzy and soon passed out.

The neighbor and I got her into bed and called the

Emergency Medical Technician. The last thing he did was check her eyes. I'll never forget what he said, and I'll be forever thankful to him. He looked up at me and asked, "Are you ready for this?"

I thought, "Oh! My God! This is not a digestive upset. This is it!" Then, out of nowhere, I said, "Mom, Mom, today is the day you'll be with Daddy and Michael again!" (Michael was the four-day-old infant she'd lost.) The words and the joy with which I said them, were completely spontaneous. That is not my belief, but it was hers. Some part of me wanted her to hear those words, if she still could hear, and I believe that she could. I was able to be by her side, caressing her and telling her how much I loved her as she died gently and peacefully, a blessing for both of us.

Beth smiled as she related the story of her mother's peaceful last years. She was quite contented that she was able to provide her mother with the experience she wanted to have. It appears that doing so nurtured something in Beth, as well as in her mother. Her mom seemed accepting and ready to die; she'd been able to live in her home, enjoy her breakfasts, and sit by the ocean.

AFFIRMATIVELY ANSWERING UNIVERSAL QUESTIONS

Part of the process of finding peace and acceptance is discovering affirmative answers to two universal questions: Was I loved? Did my life matter? These questions might be stated in a variety of forms. We can more easily accept life in its present form, when we can answer those questions positively.

Elders may not ask these exact questions. The sensitive listener will hear them even if they're not asked directly. For example, Roz's father asked why people loved her mother so much. She heard, "Am I loved?" She told her father that he was and what she loved about him. He could relax knowing that, he, too, was loved.

Discovering that their lives mattered is another task for elders as they navigate their mature years. It can be quite difficult to value our own accomplishments. They may seem ordinary and mundane. Appreciating what we have contributed is not pride; it is part of telling our whole life story.

Many who shared stories with us reported elders' comments about their "ordinary lives;" they said that they were nothing special. They didn't appreciate what they had accomplished. Asking questions from "The Getting to Know Them Better" section in chapter 2 might help elders acknowledge their accomplishments.

We have included some questions at the end of this chapter that will also contribute to a positive life valuation. This kind of inquiry helps our elders and dying loved ones know their lives are worthwhile, and that they are loved. Kaye's story is especially noteworthy because she was able to facilitate her father's life review even though he had dementia.

Kaye's Story: Finding Value Beyond Dementia: Conversations with My Father

I sat with my eighty-nine year old father for three days as he was dying. He had always been a "hale and hearty" man, but dementia and complications from a heart attack were clouding his world. In those last days, Dad was not in great pain and came in and out of consciousness. When he awoke, he was confused and very frightened because he did not know where he was. It was important to stay with him at all times.

Dad's short-term memory was failing, and in the past few years, he had developed behavior that was sometimes difficult. He repeated certain questions or comments every few minutes. It was obvious he was aware that something was wrong. He became very anxious and dependent, which was a total reversal of behavior for him.

As I sat with him, I tried to comfort and assuage the fear and confusion. Yet, his memory bank was rich and full. Through our conversations, I asked him to reflect on his life. Doing so seemed to calm him.

His life stories had always been inspirational. Of course, I knew his stories. I'd heard them many times over the years. Dad had suffered child abuse and was on his own from the time he was 11 years old. He had an amazing life that demonstrated human beings' incredible resilience. In these conversations, I asked him to reflect on the positive outcomes through the frame of appreciation.

I asked him to tell me about his childhood, about the people he was drawn to, and how they had influenced him. I asked him to reflect on times that brought him new learning. I asked him to share his early life goals and how they had changed over the years.

His response was touching. He wanted to have a family, to be a stable provider, and to be a protector of his children, none of which he had experienced as a child. He had done well in achieving these goals.

I asked Dad to talk about what he loved most about his life, his work, his family, and his friends; what had brought him joy. "Your Mother, my children, nature, and rocks!"(Dad had been a "rock hound" most of his life.) He answered readily. Other times he would take a moment to be quiet and reflect before talking. He was thoughtful and did not hesitate to share his ideas, experiences, and feelings. The remembering made him sigh and lie back, seemingly at peace. The remembering kept the dementia at bay.

He struggled most when I asked him to examine his gifts and his legacy. At those times, I shared stories of how he had influenced me and others. We talked about what wishes he would make come true for us (his family) if he could.

Together we affirmed that he had lived a purposeful life. I reminded him that his love and legacy would never die and would always be with me. The experience was life-affirming for me as well as for him. His legacy does live on with me.

Kaye felt sure that her father died with a sense of peace, knowing that his life mattered. She asked her dad to review his life when he came to consciousness, even in the last few days of his life. She helped him to articulate what he had contributed and how he had loved his family. Those long ago memories were in tact; dementia had not erased them.

COMPLETING UNFINISHED BUSINESS

Unfinished business refers to those issues and relationships that nag us, and remind us that something is missing, not complete, or as it should be. When we attend to these situations and people we are more likely to be at peace. We often think of dealing with unfinished business at the very end of life. However, taking an inventory of unfinished business, and addressing what needs to be tended to throughout life leads to more peace and fulfillment. For our purposes we are defining two categories of unfinished business: unfulfilled wishes and dreams, and forgiveness.

Fulfilling Wishes and Dreams

If we invite elders to explore the meaning of their lives through a set of questions we've prepared, they might discover unfinished dreams and have time to address them. We might help them to fulfill those wishes. Sometimes the unfinished business relates to relationships. An adult daughter, Joan P, tells the next story. She wanted something more from her relationship with her mother. We might assume from the ending that her mother also dreamed of a more loving connection.

Joan P's Story:
The Gift of Persistent Presence and Love

I was the oldest; Mom always wanted something from me, and I wanted something from her. Neither of us got what we wanted, and we were always in an adversarial relationship. I think we both wished for more.

It was hard to talk with her about anything in my life because she responded with a story about something in her life. She never listened to me. The saddest part for me is that she never knew me, as I would like to have been known. It still makes me sad.

As she got older, she became this sweet little old lady, and we got along okay. Yet, I still never felt she was interested in my life. For example, on one of her early hospital stays, I walked into her room and she just looked at me. She didn't smile or acknowledge me. It was as if I wasn't there. My dad walked in, and she smiled. That touched off something in me; it was typical of our relationship. She was in decline for two years before there came a time when we knew she couldn't survive. It lasted two weeks. As my mother was dying, I wanted to do everything possible because I didn't want to have any regrets. I was even more determined because of our history.

Those last two weeks were so intense; it was as if nothing else existed. I wasn't working at the time, so I could stay with her. It was my intention to take care of my mother. Strangely, it was she who gave us a gift. Mom became accepting and loving of everybody, including me. We took care of her, and she loved being taken care of. She didn't resist at all.

Mom created this environment of love; it was her final gift to me. I know she did it: where else might the pervading sense of peace and acceptance have come from? I had not experienced that kind of feeling before. It was as if I was just in the flow and fully present. It's as if nothing else existed. All I could think of was pure love, the spirit of God. It made me not afraid of death anymore.

Joan P. was determined. She didn't give up her dream of a loving relationship with her mother. She wanted to know she'd done everything she could to make her mother's last days loving and comfortable. Her mother made the shift that is often associated with dying. We can only assume that she gained a new perspective on her life and changed her behavior. Apparently her mother finally recognized Joan's love and reciprocated. It appears that both found the loving relationship they most wanted.

Six months after her mother's death, Joan P. took a job as a hospice nurse. She states: "I think I went into hospice as a direct result of this experience. As time goes on, I miss her more, which is interesting. It's not that I miss what I didn't have so much as I miss hearing her voice. Isn't that odd?"

Forgiveness

Forgiveness is not about condoning behavior, especially if it was violent and has hurt others. It is not even about forgetting what was done or said. It is about coming to acceptance. To do so, letting go is required – letting go of our resentment, hurt, and anger. These feelings sit like a rock upon our hearts, and they weigh us down. When we are filled with negative emotions toward others, we are less able to fully love and accept ourselves or anyone else. So forgiveness is a gift to the one doing the forgiving.

The next story is about a family that was estranged for decades. As Lucille reached out with love to her uncle, both were able to give and receive forgiveness and love.

Lucille's Story: Just in Time Reunion

Even thirty-five years later, I can still feel the anguish of being told at the age of 10 that my favorite Uncle Charlie did not want much to do with his only sibling, my mother, or her family. There had been little contact over the next thirty-five years.

Although Uncle Charlie cried on the phone at the news of my mother's passing, he did not attend the funeral or even send flowers or a card. My belief that my uncle did not genuinely care about us or me was reinforced. Over the years prior to her death, my mother spoke bitterly of her only brother and how he had given up his true family because we were "not good enough" for the family he had married into.

When I was 54, I decided I wanted to find him, but I wasn't sure how. I went on the Internet, and my first search was successful. I called his home many times to no avail. Finally, my cousin, his daughter Janet, answered and was delighted that I called. She told me that he was in a nursing home and was seriously ill.

Janet cried and told me how sad and sweet her father was, how much he regretted letting go of his sister and family. And how he was about to die feeling so much guilt and sorrow about the way he had treated his sister. She gave me his phone number.

It was an act of utter bravery for me to hold onto the phone. "Hello, Uncle Charlie. This is your niece Lucille."

The sweetest, most tender voice replied, "Oh, my baby, my baby, where have you been?"

I made a surprise visit. I walked into his room and found that, at 85, my uncle was still handsome. He was thin and frail, but with a full head of white wavy hair, and he was impeccably dressed. He looked up at me as if emerging from a fog, trying to decipher what was in front of him. He wept. I hugged him. We both wept. I told him I loved him and how I had missed him. He replied softly, "Me, too."

We spent a delightful two hours together looking over old photographs and reminiscing. He allowed me to wheel him outside. It was only later that I learned he had not left his room until that day.

The next day I went back. We talked some more, and I took him on another walk. He asked me about my mom and how she died. He started to cry and said, "I'll never forgive myself because I didn't get to see her in the last years of her life. I'm a terrible brother."

I said, "No, I'm here right now because I know she wants me to be. This is a chance for you to let go of her and for you to know that she still loves you. We both cried, and he hugged me. I knew he only had a little bit of time left, so we probably wouldn't see each other again.

Before I left, my uncle asked me to call him when I arrived home. "I want to know that you are safe." When I got back to Maine, I called. He said, "Oh, my little girl, you are safe." I got off the phone and cried. All the years growing up, my own father had never said anything like that to me. Uncle Charlie had given me the gift, even for an afternoon, of knowing what it was like to have a real dad.

It was touching, real, and very deep. Over the next few weeks, I called him frequently and sent him packages of fresh fruit. After we talked, I would always speak to Janet. She said that in the last years of his life, she'd never seen him so vibrant.

Right before Christmas, he died. My cousin called and said he'd died peacefully. She told me that there was a difference in him after my visit. I know I was supposed to see him – not just for him, but for me, too. We both got something that had been missing in our lives.

Lucille decided that she preferred to forgive her uncle for abandoning his family – and her – rather than let him die before they had an opportunity to reconcile. She asked herself the questions: Can I reconnect with Uncle Charlie even after all of these years? Is he interested? She knew she wanted the relationship, was ready to forgive, and would take the risk. If she had not made the first move, she and her uncle would have missed a valuable experience of love and reconciliation. If she hadn't persevered and searched for her uncle, she would never have known how much she was loved. Forgiveness was the path.

⸻

Anyone who has been with elders and dying people who are not at peace, have seen their turmoil and suffering. Pain is magnified. Comfort is difficult to come by. Addressing unfinished business and affirmatively answering those universal questions enhances the later years of life. If we engage elders and dying loved ones in conversations that help them to master these tasks of aging and dying, we are doing a valuable service. Everyone benefits.

QUESTIONS AND CONVERSATION STARTERS FOR FINDING PEACE AND ACCEPTANCE

Life Review:
Affirmatively Answering Universal Questions

The questions in this section explore pivotal life events, significant turning points, inner strength, and learnings from challenging times. These conversations and stories help storytellers identify important experiences, events, and decisions that have contributed to finding purpose, worth, and meaning in their lives. Answering these questions helps elders and dying loved ones recognize what they have achieved and to know that they are loved.

> **Important Contribution:** As you look back on your life, think about and share some of the contributions you have made that you are most proud of. Don't be humble. You might have contributed to family, work, community, etc. Please tell a story about it.

Follow-up:
- What is that contribution?
- What skills and knowledge were involved in making it?
- What do you value most about this contribution?

Value about Yourself: Without being humble, tell a story that illustrates what you value most about yourself as a person? What is an essential part of you that makes you who you are? It is something you value deeply and one of your core qualities or characteristics.
Follow-up:
- How has this quality influenced your life and relationships?
- How has this essential aspect given you the strength to meet challenges?
- How have others appreciated this quality or skill of yours?

Other's Feedback and Appreciation: Over the years others have indicated ways they value and appreciate you. It may have been difficult to accept or take in what they said. Would you reflect on times people have tried to tell you how much you mattered to them, and tell a story about one of them?
Follow-up:
- What do you value most about this feedback?
- Do you recognize this quality, characteristic, or skill in yourself?
- How has the ability they acknowledged made a difference in your life?

Turning Points: Would you tell a story about a turning point in your life, a time that changed your direction?
Follow-up:
- What happened and who was involved?
- What decisions did you make and how did you make them?
- How did your life change because of this turning point?
- What did you learn from this experience?

Learning through Adversity: Times of adversity often offer opportunities for tremendous personal growth and self-discovery, if we are open to the lessons. Describe a time of great personal growth born of adversity in your life.
Follow-up:
- What happened and what did it challenge you to do?
- How did it change how you see yourself?
- What did you learn that you've applied to other situations or could apply now?

Gift for Future Generations: Imagine it is twenty years from now and your grandchildren are talking about you, the grandparent who has inspired an important value or accomplishment in their lives. Imagine what you would hear if you could eavesdrop on that conversation and hear something that pleases you. What are they saying about you?
Follow-up:
- What would you most hope they would say about you?
- What legacy are you leaving?
- What is important to you about leaving that legacy?

Unfinished Business: Wishes and Dreams

Unfulfilled Dream: As you think back on your life, you probably had many dreams and wishes – some you lived into, some you didn't. Would you tell me about one dream or wish that has gone unfulfilled, and how you imagine your life would be different if it had been fulfilled?

Follow-up:
- What is important about that wish or dream?
- What reward would you receive if you could fulfill it?
- What is one thing you can do now to fulfill at least one part of that dream?

Reconnecting with People: As time goes by we lose contact with people who were important to us. Sometimes certain people made a major contribution to our lives. Yet we never voiced our appreciation. Are there people that you would like to contact and renew your relationship? If so, who are they?

Follow-up:
- What would be important for you to tell that person?
- Is there anything you want or need to hear from them?
- What would renewing that connection mean to you?

Hopes for Being Remembered: What do you most hope others will remember about you? What strengths, values, and characteristics do you hope will remain in others' minds even when you are gone?

Follow-up:

- What is important about those memories to you?
- What lessons or gems of wisdom are embedded in those memories?
- How would you feel if you knew others would remember those things about you?

Unfinished Business: Forgiveness

Forgiveness: Imagine that forgiveness is about us being clear and letting go of negative emotions that drain our energy. It's not about changing another's behavior. It is not about judgment and blame. It is about us letting go of our negative feelings and possible desire for revenge. Who in your life, or gone from your life, would you need/want to forgive or ask forgiveness from?

Follow-up:

- What or who might you be willing to forgive?
- What do you and the other need to do to mend and nurture your relationship?
- What is the first step toward achieving peace with that person or situation?

Chapter 5

CREATIVE AND POSITIVE AGING

Some find ways to age well, appreciate their lives, and remain vital. They override the culture's images and messages about aging and create their own reality. Disease, decline, and degeneration are the pillars of the outdated story; it is a debilitating one. Most of us live in a society that defines aging as a time of losing mental, physical, and emotional abilities. We suggest that while acknowledging some of the challenges, it is essential to seek the affirmative, appreciative ideas, images, and experiences of aging; then live every day to its fullest.

The culture's negative images about aging can disturb even those of us who are aging well and making the most of every day. Those outdated messages seep in and cause us to question and be fearful. Being mindful of our language allows us to embrace a new, more exhilarating image of aging. The next story is a reminder to pay attention to our thoughts and conversations. They may reveal anxiety about aging, even as we intend to stay positive and appreciate each day.

Roz's story: Facing Aging

When Roz enters a room, her smile warms everyone. She is active in many different aspects of life: She goes to the gym three times a week, plays bridge and Mahjong weekly. She is active in her spiritual community where she drums and attends classes and services. She participates at Osher Life Long Learning Institute, a senior college, where she is a student and leader. Some of her essays and photographs were published in "Reflections," the senior college's magazine. A photograph she took was chosen as the cover of the Fall 2010 issue. A meal at her house is a real treat. She travels throughout the country to visit her five children and many grandchildren. She is healthy and always seeking challenges to help her grow. Most would assume she is twenty years younger than her actual age.

Yet, Roz has been feeling anxious and not quite herself for a couple of months. She did a personal inventory and still couldn't identify the cause of her disquiet. She meditates and one day while sitting, she finally got a message. She has one of those decade birthdays coming up, and it terrifies her. She engaged in spiritual counseling and sought life coaching. She wanted to confront death and her feelings about it. She talked honestly with her women's group about her fears and anxiety.

She confided in one of her daughters, Marion. When four of the five siblings were together they talked about their mom's concerns and sent her a message via Marion.

"Mom, you took great care of us as we grew up and still do. We want you to know it's our turn. We want to do that for you."

Roz smiled as she relayed that message. Yet, she is clear. The fear and concerns about aging stick with her. She will continue to explore and face them. She wrote, "I also think the search for peace within never really ends. Everyone is a work in progress, hopefully."

The culture's value on youth and the taboo about talking of death takes its toll even on someone like Roz. Fortunately, she is actively facing the symptoms and is willing to acknowledge the source of her anxiety. She is committed to an on-going exploration of her concerns while living a full and satisfying life.

———◆———

Dr. Bill Thomas,[7] a geriatrician, reminds us that most research and writing on life stages doesn't include a description of elderhood as a distinct time of life. Most developmental theories define childhood and adolescence and stop with adulthood. The implication is that after we reach adulthood, there is only decline. After a certain age there is nowhere to go but down, nothing to look forward to but death. Who

7 Thomas, Bill, MD. Keynote speech at Third National Positive Aging Conference, Eckerd College, St. Petersburg, FL December 7, 2009.

would want to consciously embrace such an image?

As elders, when we forget something, most of us immediately associate it with a "senior moment." It was enlivening to read Dr. Gene Cohen's comments on aging. He wrote, "But what moment do adolescents have when arriving home after they left for a trip to the supermarket, and realize they forgot the shopping list their mother stressed that they remember to bring? Does the so-called senior moment really reflect the defining moment for a senior any more than forgetfulness should brand an absent-minded teenager?"[8] He reminds us to wake up and pay attention to the meaning we mindlessly associate with events.

In their newsletter, *Positive Aging*, Mary and Ken Gergen write, "Comparatively little attention has been paid to the possibility of growth, generativity, and development in the last decades of life. With the growing population of older people who enjoy increasing social, political, and economic power, the willingness to accept the dark ages of aging has diminished; a more positive image of the aging person is invited."[9]

8 Cohen, Gene D., MD. "Vintage Voices: The New Senior Moment." Aging Well (Winter 2008.): page 50.

9 Gergen, M. and K. Gergen. "Positive aging: New images for a new age," Aging International Journal, Vol. 27, No. 1 (December 2001) pages 3 – 23. Quoted in http://www.springerlink.com/content/un2x9hpgew1b0pt7/

As we become aware of research, models, and stories of positive aging, our images, language, and conversations will change. It is essential that we embrace the whole story and challenge our conditioned ways of seeing the elder's world.

As our beliefs and stories about aging shift to reflect a more holistic understanding of aging, we will be able to embrace this stage of life. This concept is not a denial of issues associated with aging. It is looking at the whole picture, and interpreting the experiences from a broader frame of reference. As we begin to see the benefits of age and tell upbeat stories about elder years, our relationship with aging will change.

One purpose of this book is to encourage readers to reframe and re-conceptualize aging and what kinds of relationships are possible with their elder loved ones. As listeners engage elders in Healing Conversations, they will recognize the richness of those many years of experience and what they can learn from them. Dr. Bill Thomas has stated that, as we relate to elders as vibrant living beings, "… our own aging self becomes something we can become true to, something we can be honest with, something we can live with pride."[10]

Research can help us age well. Studies that broaden our

10 Thomas, Bill, MD. Maryland ProAging Event on YouTube, recorded at Erickson School at University of Maryland Baltimore Campus.

perceptions of what is possible and show us how to make meaning of elder experiences are now more available. The more stories we have of people who age creatively, the easier it will be to accept and adopt new images and possibilities. We will live longer and with more vitality.

The next story is about what was lurking behind the face of a then eighty-nine-year-old resident of a retirement community.

Olivia's Story:
More Than Meets the Eye (Told by Joan)

Olivia's delightful southern drawl caught my attention. Her voice stood out from all the other voices in the hall full of people waiting to be seated for dinner in the retirement community. I felt compelled to comment on the pleasure her smile and voice brought to me. She invited my aunt and me to sit with her and her friend Marge for dinner.

Olivia is just a bit of a thing. Her white cotton shirt is ironed and crisp. Every hair is in place. Her makeup is impeccable. She walks tall and straight. What is most noticeable is her smile. She looks quite sweet and demure.

She and Marge quickly started talking about the inefficient bookkeeping department of this facility. Olivia, in a sweet southern drawl, told this story: "I went to the office three times and showed them the returned checks and their invoices that continued to overbill me. Each time, they admitted that they'd billed me twice and promised to fix it. The next month's statement came, and there was the same charge. I was determined to get this taken care of once and for all."

"I went back down to the office and told them I was writing to the corporation that owns this place. They immediately took me into the president's office. He got that invoice corrected – on the spot." She told this story with a gleam in her eye. Her words and tone of voice conveyed her feistiness and made me want to know her more, so I began a Healing Conversation.

In response to questions about the highlights of her present life, Olivia revealed that although she didn't see or hear as well as she once did, she could still write on her computer.

"Do you write every day?" I asked.

"No, just when I feel the urge. One day I was ironing and thinking and just had to stop and write, 'Thoughts While Ironing.' I wrote about Ebenezers – that's what I call those times when things work out, and you know there had to be some divine intervention. The situation looked hopeless, and then something happened that saved the day, like Ebenezer in the Bible. I look for Ebenezers and thought I'd write some down. They cheer me up."

Olivia talked about the books she has written for each of her children. Each of them was filled with information she wanted them to know about her, her beliefs, her values, her faith, and about her relationship with them.
We agreed to share some of our writing via e-mail. Olivia

surprised me with the breadth of her knowledge and her ability to write. What a treasure to discover more of the whole person under that smile and southern drawl.

Seeing this very slight, quiet, and deceptively demure woman waiting for dinner gave no clue to her depth or abilities. Thank heavens her soft southern drawl was just loud enough to arouse my curiosity. Olivia gave me hope. She modeled a possibility for when I am much older and possibly sight and hearing-impaired as she is. What a discovery.

Olivia had her ninetieth birthday in June 2009 and was still smiling, writing, and traveling. When we met after her return from a trip to celebrate with her children in Colorado, Olivia said, "That is enough birthdays." I was a bit alarmed but didn't have time to engage in that conversation. Olivia died quite quickly a couple of months later.

——◆◆——

Jane, a ninety-five–year-old, deals with some physical challenges of aging, but is determined to keep going and to enjoy life. She is a wonderful example of fortitude and creativity in later years.

Jane's story:
Aging Creatively and with Spunk (Told by Joan)

My friend Darlena asked me to create a digital story[11] about her mother, Jane. She had her ninety-fourth birthday August 3, 2009. After talking with Jane and doing some preliminary recording, it was clear the theme of her story had to be creativity and aging. She agreed, and we met in her home late one morning in the spring of 2010.

When I arrived she was dressed in shades of pink – pink starched and ironed shirt (she ironed it herself), darker pink scarf, and three-inch dangling earrings. Her makeup was subtle and perfectly applied. I wondered how she'd done such a good job with her poor eyesight, but never found out. We sat at the card table where she always holds court and often plays complex games of Scrabble.

Jane has macular degeneration and told me all she could see was the outline of my head, but no details. She is in pain much of the time from arthritis. Yet she lives alone in her single-family home and has found joy while coping with the challenges. "How do you manage to live alone?" I asked.

"Have to do it, Joanie. That's it. Have to do it." She doesn't question if she can; she sets her mind to making each day the best it can be. For example, she counts cellar steps so she can wash her clothes in the basement. She is fiercely independent and wants no part of living in a retirement community. She devises creative coping strategies that allow her to live alone.

11 Moving Life Stories (www.movinglifestories.com) captures the essence of life stories and documents them on DVD with music, photos, mementos, and taped interviews.

When I called the night before to confirm our appointment, her voice was strong and upbeat. I asked what she was doing. "I was bored with TV and started playing the harmonica," she said. "It always makes me happy."

During our visit, Jane went on to tell me, "The twin brother of the boy I used to date calls me every night. We play the harmonica to each other on the phone and guess what the other is playing. We sing and talk together. It's fun."

She continued: "The other night, Darlena and a friend came and read my poetry to me. I loved it. I can't see to read it anymore. Darlena took me to the World of Poetry event in Hollywood in 1988. I have a poem published in the book that resulted from that competition. It was in a big hall; I read two of my poems on stage. One was, 'Ike and Mamie' about two ducks. The other was 'A Dog's Dilemma.' I love my titles. One I especially like is, 'A Backward Glance.'" Jane began reciting a beautiful poem about a visit to what's left of her birthplace homestead. For decades, her poems were a regular feature in the local paper.

"Darlena took me for a ride the other night about 4:30. "She said, 'I'm not going to tell you where I'm taking you.' I didn't want her to. She wants to know if my thinking material is still up there."

"We got back to Biddeford, and I recognized the cemetery where Mom's buried. Darlena turned right after it and wanted to know if I knew where we were. 'Of course, we're at the Dollar Store. We just passed the cemetery where Mom's buried, and the store is right after it.'"

"Darlena commented, 'Your senses are really keen to know we're passing the cemetery.'"

"That's the way my life goes; it's fun. I like rides but I'd rather walk. I walk a mile a day (with a walker) down the street to the bank and back."

I said, "You have found creative ways of coping."

"Have to in order to exist. Just have to," Jane concluded.

Jane smiled and laughed throughout the two-hour interview. We both had fun. She finds ways to entertain herself by singing, dancing, and playing the harmonica. She also does a lot of the yard work herself. Her personality is so inviting that she has frequent visitors. Darlena says, "Mom gets up every morning, takes her shower, gets dressed, and puts on her makeup. She's ready for company whether they come or not."

For the interview with Jane, I had prepared a number of questions, such as: What is a highlight of your life? Tell me about it. What keeps you so creative and vital? Would you share stories of some of your most valued accomplishments? Both of us were smiling and energized as we spent time together. She presented a model of a person who does not allow external circumstances to control her life. Every day she creatively makes the best possible life for herself and those who visit her, and she enjoys doing so.

As we go beyond first impressions and appearances such as wrinkles, slow movement, and walkers, we'll be able to truly see the whole person. As we engage in Healing Conversations we'll also be able to understand our own lives differently. We'll develop more positive images of what is possible for us as we age. Sometimes we see behavior that teaches us what not to do.

When we enter into conversation with our elders, everyone gains. As inquirers, we invite elders to consider their own stereotypes and beliefs about aging. Their stories remind them of their accomplishments and the skills they can use to face present day challenges. The exchange gives elders – and listeners – an opportunity to imagine a very life-affirming elderhood.

QUESTIONS AND CONVERSATION STARTERS FOR CREATIVE AND POSITIVE AGING

Positive Aging: Reframing End of Life

This section provides topics and questions around reframing elderhood. The questions explore goals, activities, and wishes for the future. These conversation starters offer the storyteller a way of identifying important experiences that provide insights and the seeds for creating the best possible future.

Benefits of Aging: Although there may be some new physical limitations with aging, there are also advantages of maturity and experience. What is better now than when you were younger? Tell me a story that illustrates the benefits of age as you have experienced it.
Follow-up:
- What are some of those benefits?
- How are you using those advantages to instill vitality and joy into your life?
- What more might you do?

Surprises: There are lots of stereotypes about aging. Tell a story that is counter to some of them, an experience you have had that defies the stereotype of aging.
Follow-up:
- What was that experience?
- What surprised and/or delighted you?
- What was necessary for this experience to be possible?

Still to Learn or Do: If you had all of the resources, ability, and time needed, what one more thing would you like to learn or do? It might be related to something from the past that you'd like to build upon or there may be something totally new you'd like to explore.
Follow-up:
- If you learned or accomplished this, what difference would that make to your life?
- What is one step you could take now to make that experience possible?
- What would you need in order to take a first step?

Dreams: Throughout our lives we have many goals and dreams; some we achieve and some remain dreams. Would you share a goal or dream you had, whether or not it became reality? What was it and why was it so important to you?

Follow-up:
- What about that goal or dream appealed to you?
- How did it turn out?
- Whether or not it became reality, how did it contribute to your life or that of others?

Important Wishes: Imagine you have a magic wand and could have any three wishes you most desire. What are those three wishes? What would your life look like if those dreams were fulfilled?

Follow-up:
- What would you be doing differently if those wishes were reality? How would your life be better?
- What elements of these wishes are present in your life now?
- What's one small step you could take now to bring your wishes more fully to life?

Chapter 6

CONVERSATIONS
AFTER A SERIOUS DIAGNOSIS

In this chapter we address conversations after the diagnosis of a serious illness that may be life threatening. Even if we suspected such a diagnosis, these confirmations catch us off guard and shock us. Having conversations with loved ones after a diagnosis is a journey in uncharted waters for most of us. Many wonder what to say or do that would be helpful; we need support and guidance.

As people live longer, the chance of facing serious health challenges increases. They may or may not prove fatal; however, they change people and their lives. Many diseases that were once considered death sentences are now manageable chronic conditions, and others are curable. Even dire diagnoses are usually given with hope and a degree of uncertainty of outcome.

Not knowing the outcome is stressful, yet it provides hope for recovery and a continued life. It is unlikely that that life will be the same after a serious diagnosis. The experience forces us to face our fragility and mortality even if there is a full recovery. Caregivers' attention and willingness to be present and listen, supports people with diagnoses and also helps them to cope. The conversations we suggest in this chapter are meant to be supportive during the process of coping with the illness and whatever outcomes emerge.

WHAT DOES SUPPORT LOOK LIKE?

Being the support person for someone diagnosed with a serious illness requires a particularly sensitive, thoughtful listener, who is able to attend to the other. At the same time, listeners need to deal with their own thoughts and feelings. It is best for listeners to give themselves some time and space to catch their breath after they first learn of the diagnosis. Serious illness is an intrusion into life; the uncertainty of outcomes unsettles all of us.

Listeners must be aware that the upsetting news is a jolt to their systems and be compassionate with themselves as they step in to support the person with the diagnosis. When listeners deal with their own feelings and have time to recover from the shock, they will be more available to be present with loved ones.

It takes courage to open the conversation with a person

who has been given a serious diagnosis. We are in unfamiliar territory. There are so many unknowns: How will they respond? What feelings of our own might come up? Can we handle the intensity of the situation? What lies ahead?

We must be willing to walk through the discomfort of not knowing what to do and not knowing what to say before we gain a level of comfort with the situation. Commitment to the relationship enables us to stay in the room and grow through the awkward times. As we search for the courage to face our own discomfort and remain steadfast in our commitment to our loved ones, we become truly supportive. Our ability to deal with life's challenges increases.

The emotions, attitudes, and thoughts we bring to conversations make a difference. Even if we are trying to hide our feelings, they do come through. What we feel and believe sends a subtle message, even if unvoiced. Be sure you acknowledge your feelings, and do your best to match verbal and non-verbal messages.

ADVICE FROM ONE WHO'S BEEN THERE

Dr. Jill Bolte Taylor's stroke experience educates us about the subtleties of our energy and unspoken messages, and the affect they have on others. She was a thirty-seven-year-old Harvard-trained brain scientist when she had a stroke. The gift in her misfortune is that she was able to recall and write about it so we have insight into one patient's experience.[12]

Immediately after Dr. Taylor's stroke, she had no ability to use language or remember her past; her recovery was questionable. In her silenced state, she wanted to yell out to people, "I'm in here. Come find me." She described the horror of people rushing at her, demanding she give answers, and generally overwhelming her. Her admonition: "Be responsible for the energy you bring into the room. Make eye contact. Touch the person."[13]

She advises us to be present and remember we want to connect with the patient in a way that allows them to feel safe and supported. Imagine how you might do that. Would you be silent? If you speak, what tone of voice would you use? Would you move slowly and touch gently? Remember that the essence of the person you know is still there behind the mask of lost capacity and decline.

12 Bolte Taylor, Jill. My Stroke of Insight. NY: Viking, 2006. Also see her story on TED.com.
http://www.ted.com/talks/jill_bolte_taylor_s_powerful_stroke_of_insight.html
13 Bolte Taylor. Page 75.

EARLY CONVERSATIONS:
MAKING SENSE OF THE DIAGNOSIS

When we begin conversations shortly after the diagnosis, both parties are dealing with uncertainty, confusion, and shock. How do we make sense of what we've heard? What does it mean? What are we to do? The one with the diagnosis and his or her loved ones are filled with questions and have little clarity at first. As supportive listeners what is the best course of action? Listen, ask questions, and allow the person diagnosed to take the lead.

People make sense of information differently. Discovering the best way to support them means listeners need to recognize that not everyone processes information the same way. Some people need time alone to digest the news, and they aren't able to talk until they have come to grips with the implications of the information. They need to have some sense of mastery over the topic before sharing. Being a silent presence is most reassuring with people who process this way.

Other people gain clarity by talking to someone. As they hear themselves talk, they begin to come to terms with the news and to make sense of it. Talking, no matter how disorganized and rambling, is their way of understanding what they think and feel. They may be able to clarify their questions as they think out loud. Again a listening presence helps. Listeners can also ask questions to help clarify what they've heard and what loved ones are thinking and feeling.

Since we all have different styles of processing information, the empathic listener will look for signs that indicate the preferences of the loved one. The rule of thumb is to take time to listen as loved ones discuss their situation or ruminate in silence. Listening is most helpful. Well placed clarifying questions can help the person reflect and share their thoughts and feelings.

CONVERSATIONS ABOUT CARE, CRITICAL DECISIONS, AND LIFE CHOICES

Decisions about treatment, or even no treatment, need to be made after a diagnosis. Some know and accept that they have a disease that could be fatal. They recognize that they have to make life and death decisions and do everything they can to heal. Some are willing to undergo any treatment that has a possibility of curing them or giving them more time. They seek out alternative approaches and engage in them. Others do nothing.

As listeners use affirmative questions and connected listening skills they can assist loved ones to make difficult choices.

As caregivers, it is *not* our prerogative to presume we know what is best for anyone else. We might ask questions, listen, and engage our loved ones in conversation to help *them* clarify *their* desires. The most loving thing we can do is encourage them to make their own choices – even if they are not the ones we'd have made.

Dr. Susan Block, a palliative care physician, believes that, "about two-thirds of patients are willing to undergo therapies they don't want if that is what their loved ones want."[14] It helps if, at every decision point, we ask ourselves, "Is this what I think is best, or do I have evidence that it is *my loved one's preference?*" It is the loved one's decision that matters. It is his or her life. We may think a different choice is better but that is not our decision to make – unless the dying person is no longer capable of making choices.

Joan's story: Dad's Terminal Diagnosis

I learned an important lesson about the wisdom of patients and their ability to make the best decisions about treatment when my father was diagnosed with terminal liver cancer. He was in pain because of a large tumor. The doctor was clear: Dad was going to die. He could choose chemotherapy or let nature take its course. The doctor

14 Gawande, Atul. "Letting Go: What Should Medicine Do When It Can't Save Your Life?" The New Yorker. (August 2, 2010): page 49.

predicted that chemotherapy would give him a year.

I had nothing but horrible images of the effects of chemotherapy treatment, and I was sure, I didn't want Dad to go through that agony. I didn't have any doubt about the best choice. No chemotherapy! Thank goodness I didn't speak my mind. Instead, I listened to an overriding inner voice that counseled me to be quiet.

Dad chose chemotherapy. He would have three-day hospital stays spaced three weeks apart. I was determined to be there for him, so I drove from Maine to Delaware. I walked into his hospital room shortly after the first treatment and was shocked. He was sitting up, his color was good, and he looked better than I had seen him in a couple of months.

He was never sick from the treatment. In fact, it shrank the tumor and relieved his pain. He lived a year and did what he wanted. He did needed maintenance on the house, put their finances in order, and went on some trips to favorite places, all valued and important activities for him. In that year, we had the opportunity to have conversations and experiences we hadn't had before. I am so glad he made the decision he did.

Listener silence was the best choice in the above story. My dad made his own decision rather quickly. It proved to be a wise one that allowed us to have special time together. We would have missed important conversations and experiences if I had made the decision or pressured him to do what I "knew" was best.

I learned a lot about my own assumptions and how wrong they can be. This experience with my Dad taught me to recognize that what I believe strongly, even if there has been lots of proof that I am right, may not be best. This experience was an important lesson in learning to sit back and listen to the one with the diagnosis.

———••———

Conversations about the loved one's preferences, wishes, and values concerning the illness can be challenging to initiate. However, the information they provide is vitally important if the listener is to be supportive.

These conversations include a variety of topics. Some have legal implications. Talking about advance directives such as DNR, living wills, and legal designees is necessary. Although these are outside of the scope of this book, the same kinds of inquiry and listening skills make these conversations easier and more productive.

Whether or not you are the legally designated decision maker, conversations about these very delicate topics are a must. In a *New Yorker* article, Dr. Susan Block, a palliative-care physician,

15 Gawande, Atul. "Letting Go: What Should Medicine Do When It Can't Save Your Life?" The New Yorker. (August 2, 2010): page 47.

shares the story of this kind of conversation with her father.[15]

He was a seventy-four-year old professor emeritus facing surgery that could leave him a quadriplegic. She told him, "I need to understand how much you're willing to go through to have a shot at being alive and what level of being alive is tolerable to you." He was clear and definitive: life would be worthwhile if he could eat chocolate ice cream and watch sports on TV.

The time came when Dr. Block had to make a critical decision for her father. She was relieved that he had set the criteria so she was not left with the weight of deciding for him. He lived a productive life for another ten years.

Because her father's criteria and values were so clear, Dr. Block knew what to do in the time of crisis. A critical decision about his life and treatment was relatively easy because of her father's clarity. Others would have had a very different set of criteria; it doesn't matter. What's important is to know the loved one's preferences.

—————

When the loved one is about to undergo a procedure that could be dangerous, it is a natural time to ask him or her what constitutes a life worth living in case something goes wrong. These conversations give loved ones an opportunity to think about and articulate choices they may not have considered or talked about. It also provides information for family members and the legally designated decision-maker so that decisions conform to the wishes of the loved one.

As people live with disease and treatment, the outcomes become clearer. However, death as an outcome often remains uncertain for a long time. Will they or won't they live and for how long are the most important questions. In this time of uncertainly everyone is engaged in the dance of hope and acceptance.

DANCE OF HOPE AND ACCEPTANCE: HOLDING ON AND LETTING GO

The transition from fighting for a cure to accepting death is a difficult one. How long it takes varies with each individual. The shift is a process that is usually defined with starts and stops and is not a straight line – it is a dance. Many conversations come before recognition, acceptance, and peace can be attained. We call this process the dance of hope and acceptance.

The quality and nature of the dance varies depending upon many factors, such as the way loved ones and their families respond to the diagnosis, their ability to complete unfinished business, and their relationship with death. After a serious diagnosis some wage war with the disease. Some who choose this path gain strength and hope from engaging in the struggle. Some die still fighting the war, and never come to peace.

Others accept that they have a disease that is usually fatal and still do everything they can to delay the inevitable. Their priority is doing whatever it takes to have more time. They may be willing to undergo pain and discomfort in hopes of gaining more days, months, or years.

Still others accept death's inevitability and discontinue aggressive treatment. They choose to live as fully as possible even while they let go of hope for recovery. They do what they can to stay active and vital for as long as possible. They are determined to make the most of each moment. For them, quality of life, rather than the number of days, is the priority. They prepare for death on their own terms and are clear about what is most important to them in this special time when everything has changed.

From news reports and his son's eulogy seen on TV, it seems as if Ted Kennedy demonstrated the third approach. Senator Kennedy died at the end of summer in 2009. After his diagnosis of brain cancer, he used his considerable resources to find the best doctors and treatment, but there came a time when he surrendered and let go.

He knew death was inevitable and wanted to spend his limited time doing what he loved with his loved ones. Surrender did not mean passivity. He continued to lobby other legislators to pass the health care bill, a piece of legislation important to him, and spent as much time as he could onboard his beloved sailboat. At his funeral one of his sons spoke of the important summer they'd had together sailing and engaging in meaningful conversations. Senator Kennedy presents a vital picture of "a good death", one with peace and acceptance.

After the diagnosis of a serious illness, one that is possibly fatal, it is very difficult to balance the need for hope while recognizing the gravity of the situation. Healing Conversations can support those involved to explore their options, values, and feelings.

If conversation partners have previously talked about death, dying, and the value of life, this conversation is easier. If the topic is new to the conversation partners, some prompting and inviting by listeners might ease the way for the loved one. This special time is one for caregivers to ask questions and listen, listen, listen.

QUESTIONS AND CONVERSATION STARTERS AFTER A SERIOUS DIAGNOSIS

Initiating Conversations after Diagnosis:

Maggie Callanan and Patricia Kelley, two hospice nurses who wrote a classic in the field, *Final Gifts*,[16] make suggestions for starting conversations after a diagnosis. Their questions are helpful whether the illness appears to be fatal, is life threatening, or may be treatable. They suggest starting with something like, "Can you tell me what's happening?" That simple invitation may help you both get started. Additional conversation openers they suggest might be:

- I'm here when you want to talk.
- That was difficult/shocking/disturbing news. (You might take their hand, giving a silent invitation to talk.)
- I am sorry.
- I love you.

16 Callanan, M, and P. Kelly, Final Gifts: Understanding the Special Awareness, Needs, and Communications of the Dying. NY: Bantam Books, 1997.

It helps to have some questions in mind to help initiators over the first awkward conversations. Below are suggestions that might make the situation more comfortable for you.

Making Sense of the Diagnosis: Any serious diagnosis is scary and raises many questions, thoughts, and feelings. Talking and sharing can help. What are you experiencing? *Follow-up:*
- What questions do you most want answered?
- How might those answers be helpful? What would you do with the information?
- If you had access to any medical expert what questions would you like to ask?

Support: Support takes many forms and looks different to everyone. Would you tell me a story about times when you've felt supported during an illness or at other times? *Follow-up:*
- What did the person or people do to help?
- What didn't they do that was also supportive?
- I want to support you. What can I do?

The next questions might be helpful for loved ones who have been living with their diagnosis for a while. They offer an opportunity to reflect on their situation.

> **Challenging Times:** During challenging times there are opportunities for self-discovery, personal growth, and learning. As you think about this illness, what are you discovering about yourself?
> *Follow-up:*
> - What strengths are you recognizing in yourself? Your support network?
> - How has your outlook shifted?
> - What are you learning about how you successfully deal with difficult news and situations?
>
> **Making the Most of this Time:** Facing a serious illness is a wake-up call. Recognizing that life is finite reminds us to pay attention and make life-giving choices. What is most important to you at this moment?
> *Follow-up:*
> - Based on what it is you value – what actions, decisions, choices, and risks do you want to take now?
> - How will making that decision or choice keep you focused on what's most important to you?

Connecting with Family, Friends, and Loved Ones: During significant life changes, we often reach out to those closest to us. They would want to know what is happening, and you would benefit from their support. Think about the people in your life – family, friends, and colleagues with whom you would most like to reconnect. Who are they?

Follow-up:

- What do you want to say to them?
- What would it mean for you to reconnect with each of these people?
- How would you like to reconnect? Phone? E-mail? In-person visit? Letter?

Life and Death Decisions: If I am to best support and advocate for you in case you can't speak for yourself, you need to be clear about your wishes. What wishes do you have about your care?

Follow-up:

- What measures are you willing to tolerate in order to stay alive?
- What would be intolerable for you? Think about what would make life not worth living.

Chapter 7

LOVING THEM GOODBYE

Marcia asked me (Joan) what she could do to help as my mother was dying, and I replied, "Love Mom goodbye." Marcia said, "I felt such a sense of relief because I knew how to love someone, and I'm sure that everyone does." The experience of loving my mom goodbye profoundly impacted and reframed Marcia's experience of being with those who are dying. Now she's more confident and comfortable in those situations.

In chapter 6 we dealt with conversations after the diagnosis of a serious illness. We ended that chapter by addressing the situation when death is likely and talked about the dance of hope and acceptance. In chapter 7 we address the transition from dealing with a serious disease, to recognizing that death is the likely outcome, and we explore the special considerations once a terminal diagnosis is made.

The material in chapters 6 and 7 represents a journey and

a transition. Few people are told there's nothing more to be done when they first visit a doctor. It is more likely the person will receive news of a serious illness that requires intense attention and treatment. Over time some get well, some learn to live with a chronic disease, but some must face the fact their illness is terminal.

The journey for those with a terminal condition involves a transition from seeking a cure to accepting that death is likely. As people realize that death is approaching, everything shifts. They are automatically thrown into life reviews. Starting or revisiting the conversations suggested in the previous chapters will facilitate this review process. The questions in chapter 2, Gifts of Knowing Others Better, are particularly helpful in life review. In addition, special considerations associated with nearing death are appropriate issues for conversations. We address them in this chapter.

BREAKPOINT DISCUSSIONS

In a 2010 *New Yorker* article, Dr. Atul Gawande wrote that many Swedish doctors speak of "breakpoint discussions," which take place when loved ones and their doctors recognize that death is the most likely outcome. These discussions are a "systematic series of conversations to sort out when they (doctor and patient) need to switch from fighting for time to fighting for the other things that people value – being with family or traveling or enjoying chocolate ice cream."[17]

While the *New Yorker* article talks about doctor–patient conversations, similar ones are needed among family members. The decision to focus on quality of life rather than cure is a major one. It marks the shift from hoping for a cure toward hoping for freedom from pain and for the best possible quality of life. The priority becomes comfort and peace at end of life. The change is a major part of the dance. It marks the difference between regular aggressive medical treatment and palliative and hospice care.

Sometimes these honest conversations don't occur because patients want to protect their families. Emotions run high; hopes may differ among various family members. It may be difficult for the sick loved one and family to talk openly about the situation and choices available. The following story describes one patient's struggle with the decision to make the shift from aggressive treatment to hospice care.

The story is told from Jack's perspective; he is a hospice

17 Gawande, Atul. "Letting Go: What Should Medicine Do When It Can't Save your Life?" The New Yorker. (August 2, 2010): page 48.

volunteer. James, the patient, was unable to talk with his family. They weren't able or didn't know how to listen to him in order to facilitate *his* own decision. It was easier for him to talk with a neutral third party. Fortunately, Jack was there and listened in a connected way.

James' Story: Aggressive Treatment or Acceptance? (Told by Jack)

Doctors told James, "We might be able to buy you a year or eighteen months but beyond that we're not holding out hope. We're not close to finding a cure or effective treatment." They suggested hospice, and James was considering it, but he felt very conflicted.

The hospice where I volunteered offered to start supporting James while he made up his mind. I was assigned to drive him to and from the aggressive cancer treatments he had decided to continue while he made the decision. We talked during these trips.

James was tormented; he didn't know what to do. He said he was tired of treatment that didn't hold much hope, but on the other hand he was concerned about his family. He couldn't discuss this decision with them because they kept saying, "Dad, we really want you around." I guess most families wouldn't say, "Give-up."

He asked me, "How much do you put up with to provide for the needs of your family?" He needed someone to listen and let him work through his stuff.

A couple of times he asked me, "Have you been with people while they were dying? What is that like?" I described some of the things I'd seen. I tried to be honest without trying to persuade him one way or the other. It had to be James' own decision.

I told him that people go through the dying process in different ways. Sometimes it is beautiful. I've seen deaths where people saw friends and family from the past (those who had already died). They were lovingly released and went peacefully. Other people struggled. I told James, "You have to make sure you know what *you want*."

James was a little nervous and fearful of dying. At that point he had to decide whether he was more afraid of the prolonged treatment or of death.

It took almost four weeks before he was clear, "I've had a good life, and I don't see having the last year to eighteen months of it being torture all of the time." He spoke with his wife and his children and told them he needed to do this for himself because he didn't want to suffer any longer. He thought that with hospice care his last days could be as comfortable as possible, and he wanted them to understand. There was a lot of crying and talking.

I was his hospice volunteer and was able to continue visiting him until the end. It was as good as it could be.

Jack made it easier for James because he was a neutral third party and knew how to listen. He had no demands or vested interest. He also responded with information when James asked him if he knew what dying was like. Those of us who have witnessed another's death usually have experience that is helpful to the person facing the end of life. When we've been privileged enough to be present at non-violent deaths, we have most likely gained a sense of comfort and acceptance. Our experience can soothe the journey of another who is facing death or decisions about end of life care.

———✦———

Letting go and accepting death marks a transition in the dance that usually requires many conversations over a period of time. There may be lots of silence and some of it may be awkward. As in other Healing Conversations, the dying loved one takes the lead. The listener-caregiver asks questions and listens for the answers in a connected and compassionate way.

SPEAKING OF DEATH

It takes radical honesty to acknowledge that the loved one's disease or condition is most likely terminal. If we speak the word "death" aloud, it becomes incredibly real. Everyone may think about it, but hesitate to name it. Once "death" is introduced as a topic, the barrier of silence and denial is lifted. People are no longer separated by a secret that everyone knows but won't acknowledge. People can begin to talk more freely. Distance is bridged. Even if caregivers cannot travel the same path as the dying, they can all talk together about the journey.

We've learned a lot about conversations with the dying since Dr. Elizabeth Kubler-Ross dared to have the first ones in the sixties. That was a time when death was such a taboo word no one dared mention it. She was the first to document what we now take for granted: dying patients yearn to share their journey with another.

Dr. Kubler-Ross reported her discoveries in the groundbreaking book, *On Death and Dying* that was published in 1969. In the nineteen sixties physicians usually did not tell patients that they were dying. It was in this environment that Kubler-Ross, a rebel, pioneer, and psychiatrist, asked to interview hospitalized and dying patients. Even though she was censured for doing so, she asked these patients what they were feeling and thinking.

She found that these dying people usually knew they were dying even if no one would admit it. They were lonely, waiting, and hoping for someone to talk with them. They yearned for someone to listen to their experiences. They longed to share the dying process, their thoughts, and feelings. They did not want to travel that journey alone, isolated, and abandoned. They welcomed the conversations.

Maggie Callanan, a present day author and hospice nurse who has been with thousands of terminally ill patients, writes:

> *"I've learned that most dying people want to impart what they've learned from living as well as from the process of dying. They often want us to realize how precious life is. They want to demystify the journey for us and remove some of the fear. Finally, they are searching for affirmation that their life mattered to those who crossed their path and that they've made a difference by being here."*[8]

Engaging with loved ones, sharing their journey – thoughts, fears, experiences, and hopes – is especially important as they struggle to make sense of their waning moments. As loved ones prepare to die, caregivers focus on providing them with the best possible quality of life and an opportunity to say goodbye. It is difficult to initiate some of these helpful conversations since most of us have little experience supporting those who are dying. Caregivers are in unknown territory, and many ask, "What is most helpful to say and do?"

Even when we have built trust and found ways of talking intimately, the "D" word may still be almost too difficult to say. Callanan & Kelley suggest, "One way to begin talking

---

18 Callanan, Maggie. Final Journeys: A Practical Guide for Bringing Care and Comfort at the End of Life. NY: Bantam Books. 2008, page 120.

about death is to let the dying person know of your interest … asking, 'Are you going to be all right?' or 'Can you tell me what's happening?' may help you both get started. The first conversation usually is the most difficult; once you've broken the ice it becomes a little easier."[19]

Sometimes the patient is quite ready and willing to talk about death and the dying process, but friends or relatives are not. Finding a way for all to engage in these important conversations may take several attempts and a period of time. The following story illustrates what can happen.

Marguerite's Story: Finally Speaking of Death

I look back on six months of conversations with my dying mother as the best connection she and I ever had. She chose not to have the recommended heart surgery, and knew her time was limited. I would visit her, and over tea she would say something about dying. For many months, I couldn't summon up the courage to respond and would change the subject. Afterwards, when I walked out of her apartment, I was usually very angry with myself for not having the courage to have the "dying" conversation.

One day (over tea, of course), she started talking about dying again, and I said, "Tell me more about that." That was it – the beginning. She talked about whom she wanted to meet in heaven (her parents). She told me that she

19 Callanan and Kelly. Page 59

thought everyone in heaven was probably only a foot tall. She reasoned that so many people had died before her, God probably had to shrink everyone in order to make enough room. We both laughed.

She told me what dress she wanted to wear in the casket. I said I thought it had gotten a spot on it from my niece's wedding reception, and I would have the dress cleaned. My mother thought about that and said, "That's okay; I won't notice the spots." We both laughed again. We discussed many other things that we had never touched on before. That time was a gift for both of us. I would suggest that you trust what emerges!

Marguerite's mother used the "D" word, which was an invitation to have the conversation about death. All Marguerite had to do was stop and ask a question once her mother introduced the topic. Yet, it still took courage and intention for her to follow-up and engage in this conversation.

Other people might talk about a time when they're not here or talk about some future event they don't expect to be present for. They may comment on the deaths of others with the same diagnosis or focus more on obituaries. If caregivers listen closely, they are likely to hear invitations to talk about death. Then it is a matter of having the courage to ask a question or make a comment based on what the loved one said.

ACKNOWLEDGING DEATH:
THE BRICK WALL EXPERIENCE[20]

When loved ones are told they are dying and/or recognize that they are actually dying, everything changes. The world shifts on its axis. New steps must be learned and added to the dance of hope and acceptance. Dying people may not speak the words, but inside they know that everything is now different. They must find a way to closure, peace, and acceptance.

Kathleen Rusnak Ph.D., minister, and hospice worker with almost twenty years of experience, describes the "brick wall experience." When we hit a brick wall, all forward motion stops suddenly. There is the shock of impact. From that moment on everything is different. Rusnak writes, "The brick wall is a metaphor indicating a shift for the dying into a new spiritual reality."[21] The dying have a new set of tasks to complete if they are to die well. She defines those tasks in her book and CD's.

In addition, the brick wall experience separates dying loved ones from those who care for them. No matter how much we love the person, we aren't dying. It becomes a "they and we"

20 Rusnak, Kathleen. Because You've Never Died Before: Exploring the Spiritual
   World of the Dying. 2010. Order from: www.brickwall2.com
21 Rusnak, K. Email communication December 4, 2010.

situation. Rusnak makes the point, "the dying person is losing everything, while the caregiver is losing only the dying person. However this is not meant to minimize the loss for the caregiver, but is to show the huge and mostly unrecognized losses of the dying person."[22]

As caregivers recognize the work of the dying, they can notice when the dying person is engaged in different tasks and be able to support them. While we can't go where the dying are going, we can understand the journey and be available to the dying loved one as he or she makes it.

THE IMPORTANCE OF
HEALING CONVERSATIONS IN THE DANCE

During the period of transition and dying, Healing Conversations contribute to peace and acceptance for all. Recognizing the tasks of dying and being willing to participate as needed is part of the dance. Listening in a connected way, asking clarifying questions, and being present as the dying person does the work of dying, are ways caregivers provide support.

22 Ibid

Once the person with the diagnosis acknowledges that he or she is dying, the loved one has a new set of tasks and needs. Rusnak[23] defines a sevenfold framework for understanding that process. She defined what is so often called unfinished business of the dying person, and describes the experience from the dying person's point of view. We are collapsing her framework: *After the brick wall experience, dying people have two categories of tasks if they are to find peace and acceptance at end of life: 1) life review and 2) mourning.*

The first category of tasks, Life review and coming to terms with death, becomes urgent once people acknowledge they are dying. Rusnak believes life reviews are automatic. As people's life stories emerge, they have an opportunity to identify patterns of behavior, evaluate them, make amends, and change.

A particularly fascinating phenomenon is the change that is often seen in the last days or even hours of life. People may suddenly become more loving and may talk about topics they avoided before this time. It is at this phase that some caregivers hear, "I love you," for the first time. This experi-

23 Rusnak, Kathleen. Because You've Never Died Before: The World of the Dying (2 CD Set), Live second lecture with new and advanced material added, 2nd Edition (2 CD disks), 2005. Because You've Never Died Before: The World of the Dying. Can be ordered at: www.Thebrickwall2.com

ence is proof that we humans have the capacity to change until the very end of life. If caregivers recognize this possibility of change even in the last stages of life, they can look for cues to support it. Nancy knew this kind of change was possible and hoped that it would happen even if it seemed unlikely.

Nancy's Story: Hope For Loving Shift

My next to last visit to North Carolina was initiated by the caseworker's call to tell me my mother was being put in the nursing home complex across the street from her apartment. When I arrived in North Carolina and found Mother in the nursing home, she pointed her finger at me and yelled, "Why did you put me in here? Get me back to my home!" She made a huge scene, although I had had nothing to do with that move.

I got her out and told the staff she would not be coming back. She never thanked me; rather she continued to be abusive. After she was again settled in her apartment, I returned home to Maine.

One week later I got the call to come right back. I had told my mother that when the time came I would come and stay with her to the end. Slowly I realized she was letting me know this was that time. I took a few days to prepare for leaving home indefinitely and to prepare myself emotionally for what I thought would be an onslaught of anger.

When I arrived at her apartment complex, I saw two different neighbors who both told me, "Your mother is angry with you. Good luck." Before I entered my mother's apartment, I paused and offered up a prayer for strength and patience for me, and for peace for my mother. I hardly hoped to resolve our issues, but I could wish for a sense of ease dealing with them.

When I walked into my mother's apartment she was standing with the aid of a Hospice nurse near her bedroom door. She turned to me, opened her arms and said, "Nancy, you're here. I couldn't do this without you. I love you." The miracle had occurred.

Throughout the next 10 days she told me stories of her life, and always added, "You have been the light of my life." I had never heard these words before. She told me that many times in her last days.

The day before she died she fell asleep, and never awakened. I knew we were at peace because of all she had told me that week.

We can't know for sure that Nancy's mother's change was the result of a life review. However, it is one possible explanation for the remarkable change in behavior. We do know that this angry and bitter woman was able to change and make her last week one of joy, connection, and love.

We believe that everyone is capable of changing until the moment of death. Rusnak described conversations with dying people who were involved in a life review. She also depicted the positive behavior changes of these people as they became more loving, accepting, and at peace. The change was so dramatic it seemed like grace, a gift.

However, not everyone is open to this special opportunity to change behavior, make amends, and find peace. Dying people must be willing to reflect on their lives, acknowledge what they celebrate and behavior patterns they wish they could change. They must be willing to do the work of change if they are to make these dramatic shifts.

The second category of tasks the dying must accomplish is mourning. Rusnak describes the totality of loss the dying one faces and degrees of mourning that are likely. They will not have an opportunity to heal from their loss and go on. Their lives are ending. Their mourning may only be expressed indirectly. If caregivers listen with this possibility in mind they may be able to comfort their dying loved one.

It is through conversations, silent and verbal, that caregivers are able to support the dying. They may help them to celebrate life, clarify wishes, take action, and die peacefully. Sometimes words aren't needed. Sitting quietly together, maybe taking a hand or placing your hand on the person's shoulder, are all that is needed. The more comfortable care-givers can be with the situation the more ease they are model-ing for the dying loved one.

THE NATURE OF SUPPORT DURING THE DANCE: LET THE DYING LOVED ONE TAKE THE LEAD

Support means being available to serve the dying loved one. One task is discovering what the loved one wants and needs, then doing what you can to provide that for them. It is not about fixing this unfixable situation. When caregivers trust their loved ones to know what is best, they honor them rather than control or take over. Caregivers can make sure that loved ones have all relevant information needed to make informed decisions. Once they do, the choices belong to the dying loved one. Making those decisions is part of finding acceptance and peace and dying with dignity.

In the next section we explore what to do (and not do), what to say, and how to prepare to support the dying loved one and his or her family, defined as the extended network.

What to Do (or not do)

First, the principles of being a supportive and caring conversation partner remain the same, be present, listen to connect, and ask questions.

Sometimes what is most important is what we do *not* do. Although our initial urge may be to rush in and comfort, that is usually not the most helpful approach. Stop, watch, and listen to the person with the diagnosis before you jump into action. Doing so gives you an opportunity to listen, see your loved one's reactions, and more clearly identify his or her needs. Then you can tailor your behavior to meet the needs of that person.

Below we list some behaviors you might encounter and suggestions of what to do. These examples are based on the work of Callanan and Kelly[24] and Rusnak[25].

You may find your loved ones:

- **Staring into space or out the window and not particularly responsive.** If so, pull up a chair and ask, "What are you thinking?" Be prepared to sit and listen non-judgmentally. They may tell you about their past, what they are going to miss, and how they are feeling.

- **Stuck repeating a story about a specific incident**

24 Callanan and Kelly. Final Gifts. and Callanan, Final Journeys.
25 Rusnak. Because You've Never Died Before: The World of the Dying (2 CD Set)

or relationship. If so, know they are probably doing a life review and are immobilized by their version of a story about a person or incident. They can only see their own perspective, and it troubles them.

Ask clarifying questions. You might ask them to do some parts of the Whole Story activity found in chapter 3, "Acknowledge Multiple Perspectives" section. You might help them to reframe the situation, or ask what they wish would have happened or could happen.

- **Talking about a particular person they had conflict with or the opposite, avoiding mention of a particular person you'd expect them to talk about.** If so, realize they are probably still in conflict about this person or a situation. Talk to them about mending relationships and forgiveness and its meaning. See questions at the end of chapter 4.

- **Telling many stories about their lives, but not in a way that seems satisfying.** If so, they may be stuck in the emotions of the stories and unable to identify their own behavior patterns. You might be able to suggest *possible* behavior patterns and *question* if they fit their experience. After they name dysfunctional behavior patterns, you might talk to them about other behavior options. Ask, "What else might you do?"

- **Talking to an invisible person.** If so, remember the phenomena of "nearing death awareness" that Callanan and Kelly describe in their book, *Final Gifts*. Rusnak agrees and goes further. She believes that someone who is already dead, someone who cares about the dying person, visits *every* dying person.

These invisible visitors come to help with the transition. There are many stories to confirm her belief.

If dying loved ones speak to someone as if that person were present but you see no one, if they talk about seeing invisible people, if they have a far away look and often a smile, know they may be involved in an experience of "nearing death awareness." Assurance and validation can be comforting. Do not try to convince your loved one that the experience is a hallucination. That response is quite confusing, disorienting, and upsetting.

Ask your loved one what or who he or she is seeing or talking to. Ask for more information. Allow yourself to suspend your own reality and enter into, or at least accept, theirs. You are likely to learn a lot about their experience.

No matter what your eyes and ears are conveying, know that what your loved one describes is very real for her or him. That version of reality differs from yours. We all have different versions of the same event. This confrontation with differing realities is the same as recognizing the varied versions of reality we all have in everyday life.

Sometimes even dying loved ones have difficulty accepting what they see. They may fear that they are going crazy. Often they won't speak to anyone about what they see for fear of the other's reaction and judgment.

The phenomena of nearing death awareness became very real to Joan for the first time when she attended her dad during his dying process.

Joan's Dad's Story: Am I Going Crazy

One day during one of Dad's hospitalizations for chemotherapy, I walked into his room and found him quite agitated. I asked, "What's the matter, Dad?

"I think I'm going crazy," he stated mater-of-factly.

"What's going on to make you think that?"

Dad explained, "I keep seeing dead people."

Immediately I suspected he was engaged in the "nearing death awareness" experience that Callanan and Kelley described. I asked, "Who are you seeing? Do you know them?"

"My mother and some other people keep appearing," he responded. Dad's mother died when he was seven.

Thank heavens for the information I'd read. When I explained to Dad that he was perfectly normal and that many people facing death have this experience he settled down. "In fact," I said, "you might consider it a gift."

Callanan and Kelly described this phenomenon as one that occurs close to death. That has usually been my experience. However, Dad was seven months from death. It may be that these visitations occur much sooner than a nurse would notice. I suspect that some of Dad's peace during the last year of his life may have been based upon the visits from his dead mother. Once he knew they were a common occurrence, he could be reassured by them rather than concerned.

Whether the dying loved one has an invisible visitor, seems removed and remote, is trying to make sense of life or something else, as caregivers we are invited into the intimate process of saying goodbye, completing final tasks of the dying. It is important for us to be knowledgeable about what is possible. If not, we may immediately become concerned, suspect pathology, and do those things that are not helpful such as sedate the dying the loved one.

————◆————

In summary, watch, listen, and stay attuned to the dying person and his or her reactions. Be flexible as the situation changes. As you, the support person, tune in to your own reactions and to those of the dying person, more thoughtful and appropriate actions and conversations will arise. Over time, you will know what the loved one needs.

What to Say

In this new situation caregivers often wonder what to say. They don't want to upset dying loved ones, and yet most want to be available to talk about whatever is helpful. In her latest book, *Final Journeys: A Practical Guide for Bringing Care and*

Comfort at the End of Life,[26] Maggie Callanan makes these suggestions for caregivers. They can be helpful immediately after recognition of the finality of the situation or during the dying process.

- Describe what you see: "You look sad today. I wonder what is making you sad. If you want to talk about it I'm here."

- Clarify your concern: "I wonder what you're feeling and how I might help. Let me know if you want to talk about it."

- Acknowledge the dying person's struggle: "It must be difficult to keep facing one challenge after another. It must take lots of energy. Does it?"

- Or simply: "I'm here and I care about you."

The most supportive approach is to listen and watch instead of making assumptions. The energy of caring will be communicated on a non-verbal level as well as in words. Inviting loved ones to share their experiences, and to talk about their concerns and fears allows them to explore, grow, and find a path to acceptance.

26 Callanan, page 25

As a conversation partner what you say is almost less important than being present, and being willing to listen and engage in conversations about the difficult subjects of death, end of aggressive treatment, fears, and hopes for the active dying process. Being present with our loved ones in this situation requires us to have our hearts open, even when they are breaking.

The situation invites us to take time to focus on these more emotional and spiritual aspects of the relationship even as demands for physical care and comfort increase. As we do so, we create space for the relationship to blossom and to provide support through this intense transition. We make time for the sacred tasks of dying.

Supporting Family Members

Family members, not just the person who is dying, need support. Sometimes the person who is dying is more able to accept the situation than other family members are. When family members cling to the loved one, denying the gravity of the situation or simply unwilling to talk about it, they are holding on. Until they let go, peace is more difficult for the dying loved one. Those family members who are holding on need loving support in order to say goodbye. The next story is a lesson in patience. It shows a way to lovingly ease family members into letting go, especially when the patient is ready to say goodbye.

Marvis's Story: Easing Into Letting Go

During a phone call in January of 2000, my mother communicated her upset at my father's lack of recovery from his bouts of pneumonia. She told me that on New Year's Day, while they were eating lunch, he seemed to choke a bit and had trouble swallowing. Since then, his ability to eat or swallow, to talk, or to care for his bodily functions has not been the same. Even though my mother was upset, she declared that it wasn't anything unusual.

As I listened to her, I had a flash of intuition. My dad's system was shutting down, and it was his time to transition out of his body. I felt that we, his children, needed to be there and give him the closure he might need in order to move on. My sister and I left Tucson for Wisconsin as soon as we could book a flight.

Once there, our mother kept telling us that if they (the hospital staff) could just get him over the pneumonia, he would be okay. She hypothesized that she could bring him home and take care of him. Things would be just like they had always been.

I asked her to tell me what the doctors were telling her. She repeated their words: "They said his prognosis isn't hopeful, and that even if he could recover from pneumonia, he would have to regain his abilities to swallow, talk, and walk. And to do so with dementia, which prevents the recall and memory necessary to learn, is not a viable option." It was as if the words flowed through her but she didn't hear them.

As I listened to her recite the doctor's prognosis, I realized it was my mother who was holding on to the idea that he could get well. Maybe it was she who needed to be encouraged to let go. This suspicion was validated when I walked into my father's hospital room. I knew he wasn't going home. He was comatose, having great difficulty breathing. As I observed him I sensed peace within him.

It was then that I knew for sure: it was my mother's inability to let him go, along with her need to control things that was preventing my father from passing. My purpose for being there became quite clear. It was my role to champion my father's release from this life to the next. I felt a deep honor via a silent communication that could not be explained or described. I just felt incredibly close to his spirit.

I appealed to my mother's sense of love and compassion for him. I asked her to retell me what the doctors had been telling her. Then I'd ask, "Do you think he'll be able to remember new directions and instructions, knowing that he didn't know where his bedroom was before the stroke?" She admitted that it would be difficult.

I asked my mother why she wanted him to live when the doctors told her that his recovery was not a viable option. She responded honestly, "I don't want to live without taking care of him. If I had done things differently and made different decisions, maybe he wouldn't be facing death right now." Listening to her, I recognized her tremendous guilt. Then I could better understand her need to fight for his recovery. It would ease her sense of responsibility, and she would feel better about herself.

Each day, I asked her to look at him and ask him, "What would you like to happen, Carl?"

With time, gentle words, and many questions, she recognized that the loving thing to do was to release him from his suffering. It was okay to say goodbye to the man she loved. Even though this was hard, sad, painful, and very scary for her to do, it was the loving thing for him. She waffled back and forth, but she was eventually willing to entertain the idea that he would not be getting back to the "normal" that she remembered from a month before.

Finally she was ready, and my dad was moved to a hospice facility. Once he was settled in, I flew back to Arizona and my sister stayed with my mother. A couple of days later, Dad died peacefully after my mother and sister left his bed about 5:30 PM. He died alone. I know that he chose it that way.

Marvis realized her job was to help her mother find acceptance of her father's impending death. Patiently asking questions that required her mother to state facts and think about what her husband would want helped her mother to let go.

———

The period of saying goodbye to a loved one is a special time. It can be one of tenderness, closeness, and enhanced relationship. It is truly a gift of time. Hospice nurses often remark about the internal work dying people engage in during their last weeks or days. This period offers time to complete the tasks of living and dying. The dying review their lives, hopefully celebrate what they value about them, define what they regret, and have an opportunity for forgiveness and changed behavior. Many caregivers report seeing their loved ones' behavior become more openly loving and accepting in their last days. Their experience confirms our belief that people can change – until they take their last breaths.

Caregivers have an opportunity to say goodbye and finish any of their own unfinished business during the dying time. Conversations continue in various forms. Your questions and presence will be a gift to both of you. As they mourn you can't take away their spiritual pain, but you can be there to hold a hand and let them know they are loved. You might even be able to help them take actions needed to find peace.

If we recognize that dying is a call to the sacred, we'll be more at peace as we take the journey with our loved one. The sacred calls us to our hearts, to the wholeness of who we are, and to a renewed connection with all of those we've loved and who have loved us. It can be a time of gratitude and love. As we surrender to the process, we open our hearts. If we listen for inner guidance, we'll know how to best support and care for our loved ones on the last step of this human journey.

QUESTIONS AND CONVERSATION STARTERS
AFTER TERMINAL DIAGNOSIS

Usually after a terminal diagnosis there is time for the loved one and caregivers to come to terms with death and complete any unfinished business. After people hit the brick wall and acknowledge that they are dying, they experience a sense of urgency. It is time to review their lives, complete unfinished business, and mourn anticipated losses. This is a time when people are more open and reflective. Most are more willing to express their gratitude, love, and share more of their lives, than previously. This time and what can be done is the gift of a terminal diagnosis.

Some questions about life review, completing unfinished business, forgiveness, and fulfilling wishes have been suggested in chapter 4. They are relevant to ask the aging as well as those who are dying. In this section we add some questions that are particularly relevant as the person prepares to die.

The questions and stories in the previous chapters on getting to know them better, enhancing and mending relationships, and finding peace and acceptance, apply at this time. Those questions invite the dying person to reflect and to do a life review. However, after a terminal diagnosis, there may be additional kinds of questions to ask. Some are in the text of this chapter; additional ones are below.

Sharing this experience: Would you like to talk about your present experience? This journey can be lonely if taken alone. Sharing your experience is likely to give you a chance to sort through your own thoughts and feelings. In addition, sharing will help those of us who haven't had the experience to understand it better. If you are ready to talk about what is happening to you, I have some questions. *Follow-up:*

- What are the most important things you want me (and others) to understand about this time of your life?
- What is the experience of being diagnosed with a terminal disease like? What stands out in your mind?
- How can I/we support you at this time?
- What are you experiencing, thinking, and learning that you'd be willing to share?

Invitation to Talk:[27] When your loved one seems uncommunicative, distracted or focused else where, you might ask: What are you thinking about today? Where are you now? Then sit quietly and listen.

Completion: It is important to attend to any issues or relationships that feel incomplete.
- What do you want to say that you haven't before?
- What do you need to do so that you feel peaceful? What can I do to make that happen? What are you willing to do to make that happen?
- Who do you want to say goodbye to? Do you want to

---

27 Rusnak, K. ibid

talk to them in person, write, e-mail, or phone?
- Who do you wish you could have a conversation with? Disregard negative past, just think about the people you'd like to talk with.
- Do you have certain items you want to make sure certain people have? If so, what are they and how will you make this happen?

Anticipating Loss: You might hear the dying person talk about something or someone they'll miss. They may also seem particularly quiet and sad. If so this is one way to invite them into conversation about the losses they are mourning.
- What have you loved or appreciated most about …?
- Tell me about ….
- What are your concerns about …?
- What are your hopes for …?

Regrets: (These responses are to be used ONLY if the dying person talks about regrets. It is not up to caregivers to lead the dying loved one into an inventory of regrets.)

Mostly listen as loved ones speak of regrets. They trust you won't judge or they wouldn't be sharing. Allow them to express their pain as you stay present and witness. Don't try to make everything OK or take away their psychic pain. You can't. Allow the person to decide what he or she wants to do about regrets.

The following questions are designed to give the dying loved one an opportunity to see possibilities for change and plan some action.

- If you knew you'd be well received, what would you most like to do about the situation?
- If you had a magic wand and could go back to that situation/person what would you do differently? Listen for the response, then ask: What of that could you still do? Would you be willing to say that to the other person?
- What positive outcomes could happen if you did something different? What can you imagine doing about that situation now that you haven't done before?

Death and Dying: Are you willing to share some of your thoughts?

Follow-up:
- What is most important to you? How have your priorities shifted as a result of your diagnosis?
- What are your hopes and concerns about the course of your disease?
- What do you think lies ahead for you?
- What kind of trade-offs are you willing to make in order to stay alive?

Death and Beyond: Death is a mystery and no one knows for sure what happens. Yet, we all have our own beliefs and thoughts. Would you share some of yours?

Follow-up:
- What do you believe happens after we die?
- What are your hopes?
- Have your beliefs changed? If so, how?

Legacy: Most people hope their life has mattered and that they have made a contribution. They hope it will be recognized and celebrated. What are your hopes for a legacy? What do you hope people will remember about you and build upon?

Follow-up:

- What do you hope we will celebrate most about you?
- What kind of celebration of your life or memorial would honor you most?
- When you think of your legacy, what do you expect we'll remember and honor most? Is that what you want or is there something more?

SECTION 2

HEALING CONVERSATIONS: THE ESSENTIALS, PREPARATION, AND MASTERY

Now that you have a sense of what is possible through the stories and suggested questions in the previous section, it is time to talk about why Healing Conversations work, and how to prepare for and master the approaches and techniques described previously.

This section is divided into four chapters: 8) Essential Building Blocks: Appreciative, Energizing Questions and Stories, 9) The 1, 2, 3's of Healing Conversations: Intention, Presence, and Connected Listening, 10) Preparing for Healing Conversations: Little Things Make a Difference, and 11) Dealing with Unexpected and Difficult situations.

The information in these chapters will help you understand the underlying concepts and "how to" create your own questions. This section defines preparation and mastery of Healing Conversations. By taking time to master the basics of planned and structured Healing Conversations, you will become more adept at engaging in ongoing and spontaneous ones.

Chapter 8

ESSENTIAL BUILDING BLOCKS: APPRECIATIVE, ENERGIZING QUESTIONS AND STORIES

STRUCTURED AND SPONTANEOUS HEALING CONVERSATIONS

We have defined a structured approach to conversations in response to the many questions of "What do I say? How do I start such different conversations?" "Will they work in *my* family?" The structure builds a bridge so that people can make the leap from superficial and general conversations to more meaningful ones. Using the structure gives listeners confidence to make this shift.

When first engaging in Healing Conversations listeners gain confidence if they choose topics of inquiry and specific questions in advance. In the beginning it is often comforting and effective for initiators to write appreciative questions before meeting with loved ones. Questions in Healing Conversation have a particular form and it makes a difference in the outcome. As you practice using them, crafting appreciative and engaging questioning will become easier in the moment, and you will be able to be more spontaneous.

Whether prepared or spontaneous, Healing Conversations rely on the same structural elements: appreciative and energizing questions, stories, and connected listening. Asking genuinely appreciative questions and listening to life stories creates a bond between listener and storyteller. Conversation partners become engaged and energized.

THE POWER OF QUESTIONS

Questions get a decidedly different response from statements. Statements tell; questions invite interaction. When conversations consist mostly of exchanging opinions, people tend to become defensive. Instead of listening, they either start planning their next comment or anticipate the other's next move. A statement is usually met with another statement. The people involved often become intent upon making sure they are heard and that their point is accepted. In these interactions, people aren't listening to learn but to assert their opinions.

David Cooperrider, the originator of Appreciative Inquiry, wrote, "*Inquiry itself creates wonder. When I'm really in a mode of inquiry, appreciable worlds are discovered everywhere. The feeling of wonder is the outcome.*"[28]

When Cooperrider writes of "the spirit of inquiry," he is referring to our natural curiosity and the questions that arise from it. When we engage with a spirit of inquiry, we want to learn and explore, our minds are open and eager to discover what might emerge. We invite the other to be a companion on that journey.

Questions are powerful because they focus our attention and create a particular lens through which we view the world. They open a space for relationships to flourish as they invite another to join the exploration. They ignite imaginations and creativity.

When we ask questions with a genuine spirit of inquiry, we want to first hear and understand the other's point of view or information. Sharing knowledge, ideas, and images is likely to engage the imagination of both parties. Together, they are able to create something better than either one of them could

---

28 David L. Cooperrider. "The Child as Agent of Inquiry." OD Practitioner. (Jan. 1996) Vol. 28, page 5 – 11.

alone. In other words, the conversation adds meaning, an opportunity for creativity, and the possibility of additional options emerging.

Questions, born of genuine curiosity, fuel lively interaction. Relationships flourish when participants build on what was just said. Rather than starting a new topic, one of the partners asks clarifying or probing questions about the topic the other was discussing. Doing so expands investigation into one particular topic of interest. When people continue to ask about and comment on one topic, the exploration deepens and, together, the conversation partners create more shared meaning.

Questions are fateful and powerful. They invite others into relationship and ask them to reflect and share their thoughts, experiences, and viewpoints. Communicating in this way engages people and builds bonds. In Healing Conversations, questions are a response to a genuine desire to learn, to build connections, and to understand the other.

APPRECIATIVE AND ENERGIZING QUESTIONS

One of the basic building blocks of Healing Conversations is questions. These are not any questions, but appreciative and energizing ones. Appreciative questions are framed in the positive. So instead of asking what elders want to avoid in their living situation we'd ask, "Please tell a story about a living situation that nurtured you, brought out your best, and gave you a great deal of satisfaction?" The perspective is the half-full glass.

These questions ask about topics that are likely to engage the storyteller. Appreciative questions are designed to create meaningful connections as well as energize the storyteller. They are relational, invite deeper reflection, and are positively focused.

They usually invite storytellers to search their memory banks for the best of what they've known. Every situation has a "best" part of it, and the story of it demonstrates what is possible. Usually the images and stories that emerge are positive and invigorating. They are often peak experiences, ones the storyteller would like to re-experience. They may also be conditions they wish would occur more frequently. The stories the storyteller shares are of events and people they value. They provide cues about the storyteller's values and wishes for the present and future.

APPRECIATIVE QUESTIONS

- Are stated in the affirmative – asking what is wanted rather than what isn't wanted.
- Ask what works, what is best rather than what is the problem.
- Intentionally search for experiences of satisfaction, achievement, contribution, and joy.
- Are open-ended, evocative, and use nonjudgmental language.

Effective appreciative questions have the ability to: (1) invite dialogue and connection, (2) focus attention on what is essential and life-affirming, and (3) help us understand and appreciate each other. If we use more appreciative questions in our everyday lives, conversations and relationships will be more connecting and satisfying.

Appreciative questions reflect a desire to know the storyteller. Initiators' genuine curiosity is communicated when they inquire into storytellers' lives. When people are invited to share their stories, they are likely to respond even if they hadn't been particularly talkative in the past.

After Marcia read a draft of this book she decided to change the dynamics of family visits. She wasn't satisfied with her father's usual proforma grunt as he continued to stare at the TV in response to her "Hello, how are you?" On this visit, she did something different.

Marcia's Story: What Else Do You Want to Know?

Using some of *Healing Conversations Now's* suggested questions, I just had an incredible visit with my dad for his ninetieth birthday. He had never really responded to me. He always let my mom be the communicator for the family. He usually spends most of his time in a lounge chair flipping TV channels. This visit was different. I walked around his chair so we were face to face. Then I asked him what he remembered about some of his childhood friends whom I'd never met or heard about.

He came alive, and suddenly it was as if he was ten years old, and on the baseball diamond. He told me which buddy was playing which position. Each time he spoke of a boy on the team, he was more animated.

My mother was dumbfounded. "Alan, you never told me you played in a championship game."

He responded, "No one ever asked." With this, he turned off the TV and asked me, "What else do you want to know?" He was so energized he did something he hadn't done before – he got out of his chair, went into the kitchen, and joined in conversation during dinner preparation.

Reading the stories in this book Marcia realized there was something she could do to improve her relationship with her father. He had always appeared disinterested in conversation.

Yet, once she took the opportunity to ask him questions about his life, she discovered that he was quite eager to engage. We never really know what another might share until we ask.

—————

Questions direct attention and invite interaction. People usually think and talk about the topic of the question. If we choose topics that interest people, they are likely to engage and share enthusiastically. The next story demonstrates what can happen when we ask an appreciative question that invites the elder to engage in a topic of interest.

Nettie's Story: Energized by Questions (Told by Joan)

Nettie was extremely frail. She was in constant pain and ate little. Mostly, she stayed in bed. However, one Saturday afternoon, she rallied at the prospect of a visit from her beloved nephew, Jay, and his wife, Sandy.

Barbara and Claire, two nieces taking care of her, helped her to shower, choose her wardrobe – something extremely important to Nettie - and put on makeup. She wanted to make sure her shoes matched her dress and that her full head of white hair was turned under in a pageboy bob. She looked good although thin as a rail. Maybe her radiant smile made all the difference.

Nettie made an entrance and sat in a chair of honor surrounded by family members. This family was loving and demonstrative. They became deeply involved in a discussion of politics. Nettie usually loved this topic; however she became more and more quiet. When there was a lull in the conversation, she protested that she couldn't sit there anymore and said that she wanted to go back to bed.

Instead of responding to her request, I took this opportunity to know more about Nettie, and asked a question about her favorite family stories. Immediately, Nettie perked up and began telling stories about Jay. He was her first nephew. She spoke of times when he was a baby. She told of going to his house whenever she could. If he was asleep, she'd just sit and gaze at him. He beamed as she told stories of her devotion to him.

More stories emerged. As Nettie told stories, she became energized, and was able to continue the conversation for another hour. Finally, she asked Jay, "Can I sit on your lap?" What a sweet picture – frail Nettie enfolded in her beloved Jay's powerful arms. The question about her favorite family memory changed her focus, and it had a significant and memorable impact on the visit and our memories. It was the last time all of these people were together.

Although it would have been easy to give up and help Nettie back to her bed, everyone benefited by asking her to tell stories that were important to her. She was always an entertaining storyteller, and that part of her superseded any pain. We all heard about her devotion to her nephew, and we witnessed the love they shared.

If we want to understand another, ask appreciative questions. Appreciative questions elicit all kinds of information that might remain hidden if we didn't ask. It is difficult to resist genuine curiosity and a listening presence.

As Joan visited her aunt's retirement community, she began noticing certain residents and became curious. She asked some of them appreciative, energizing questions, and a connection was created as they shared. One example follows:

Joan's Story:
Discovering Vibrant Elders Through Questions

Maxine and Dennis invited my aunt and me to join them for dinner. He was bent forward, walked extremely slowly, and wore oxygen tubes. He barely had the strength to speak above a whisper. Although he was quiet, his eyes and face indicated that he was involved in the conversation.

I asked him about his work, and he came to life. He gave many details of his life as a Ph.D. chemist and an administrator. His mind was still sharp. He remembered lots of details. He responded to questions by telling tales of favorite activities. The couple began sharing stories of their trips to Egypt and England. Maxine inquired, "What year did we go to Egypt? Did we also go to the Holy Land on that the trip?"

Without blinking an eye, Dennis replied, "We went to England the first time in March 1967." He followed that up with many details. His eyes twinkled. As the conversation continued, he smiled and became animated.

Almost two months later, when I was back at the retirement community for another visit, Dennis called me by my first name and engaged me in conversation when he saw me in the hall. His actions were intriguing, considering that I'd never seen either one of this couple initiate conversations with anyone else.

Once again, this conversation reminded me of the delights of engaging with elders. Appearances are deceiving. If we ask appreciative questions instead of telling our opinions or assuming the other has nothing to offer, it is likely that we'll be rewarded with an invitation to share another's life. People want connection with others, but may be shy or not know how to initiate these conversations.

In Healing Conversations the majority of appreciative questions are past oriented. Once life stories and images from the elder's past emerge and are explored, we can focus on bringing those experiences and strengths into the present and future. Listeners can remind storytellers to use the resources they've defined in stories they've told about their past.

Some questions are future oriented. They ask storytellers to imagine the future, as they'd most like it to be. We ask these questions after exploring positive aspects of the past and present. Future questions invite storytellers to open their minds to more options. The responses may indicate what is missing in the present. They may also describe what is desired. Once elders entertain the possibility of a desirable future and have a realistic image of it, they are more likely to do what is required to make it a reality.

Asking appreciative questions, we are able to discover elders' wisdom and learn fascinating stories of their lives. Elders have much to teach us and are just waiting to be asked. All it takes is curiosity. It is heartwarming and inspiring to see people come alive and share their life stories.

Appreciative questions focus on the storyteller's best experiences, what they want, and what they value. These questions energize and bring forth the best of both conversation partners. Questions, but particularly appreciative ones, are a basic tool of Healing Conversations.

Sequencing Questions

Enhancing relationships is the ultimate purpose of Healing Conversations. The sequence of questions can make a difference. Usually we begin with more general questions in order to ease the conversation partner into sharing more comfortably. When some rapport has been established, we ask questions that invite more intimate conversation.

Core questions ask about high points, values, pivotal

events, and peak experiences from the past. Another kind of question is future oriented; it asks storytellers to share their hopes and wishes for the future. For additional information and a supplemental list of questions, please check our website: www.HealingConversationsNow.com.

Clarifying and Probing Questions

Follow-up or probing questions enhance clarity, meaning, and understanding. *After* the storyteller has completed the whole story, the listener may ask clarifying questions. Listeners do not interrupt. Instead, as they listen they make sure they understand the characters, activities, and meaning of the story. If not, they ask clarifying questions.

Unless your purpose is to create a genealogy, you need not focus on details of factual information. Don't correct the elder with what you believe is a more "true" version of the story. Instead, attend to the storytellers' experiences and the meaning they attribute to the situation. In Healing Conversations, we listen to information, yet our primary goal is creating a deeper understanding of the person who is sharing the story.

Probing questions request more information. They may ask the storyteller to expand on a statement or idea they've just discussed. They may inquire about something that is missing. The answers fill in gaps and add context. Added details create more understanding and make it easier for the listener to imagine being in the story. They may also connect the dots for the teller. The interaction adds shared meaning.

Often probing questions build upon something the teller has just said. Frequently probing questions repeat a bit of the original response, and ask for more detail. They help tellers to reflect on their experiences and to further explore them. For example, an elder who mentioned her favorite pet, Omar, might be asked, "Tell me more about Omar and your relationship with him."

Additionally, these questions may inquire about something that seems as if it would be in the story but is missing. An example might be asking about a relative who played a seemingly minor role in a family story, or one who was quickly mentioned in one portion of the story, but not again. You may notice that someone is missing from the story. For example, a listener might ask, "What about Sally, your sister, wasn't she around at that time?" The answer may reveal an essential family dynamic that wouldn't be discussed without probing.

Probing questions usually begin with "what" or "how." They ask storytellers to stop, reflect upon their own stories, and articulate a more complete picture or understanding of the situation or person. These "questions" can also be statements such as, "Tell me more...?" Questions beginning with "why" are seldom used because they can elicit a defensive response or a rationale rather than an exploration. People may feel put on the spot and think they need to justify something when asked why.

Some examples of probing questions and comments that invite the storyteller to elaborate include:

- Tell me more.
- What made that important to you?
- How did that affect you?
- How were you feeling?
- What was your contribution?
- How has it changed you?
- What do you value most about that experience or situation?
- What makes you most curious about that relationship or experience?
- What did you learn?

STORIES AND STORYTELLING

In Healing Conversations, we invite the loved one to respond to questions by telling life stories. Remembering and reminiscing about our positive life stories *with others*, enhances well-being. Verbal sharing and savoring of stories evokes positive feelings associated with those events and improve the experience. Reminiscing can be quite pleasurable and create a sense of contentment. It is most helpful when those reminiscences are shared rather than kept inside one's own mind. Sharing positive stories energizes the teller and helps to maintain positive feelings and health. Sharing aloud with another is much more powerful than simply writing about the events.[29]

Chronologies list events in chronological order and focus on factual data. They are emotionally neutral lists of events. They may offer valuable information, but are flat and lifeless. The information is primarily logical and linear. They are more difficult for most to remember than stories rich with details and emotion-evoking scenes.

Stories are powerful because they encompass the whole experience and invite the listener to walk in the teller's shoes. Good ones provide enough detail so that the listener can imagine being present with the teller in the story. The two truly become conversation partners. It is easier to understand the elder and the situation from a story than it is from a list of facts or events.

For thousands of years, history was passed down through

29 Lyubomirsky, S., L. Sousa, and R. Dickerhoof. The costs and benefits of writing, talking and thinking about life's triumphs and defeats. Journal of Personality and Social Psychology, 90:692-708. (2006) Sited in Lyubomirsky, The How of Happiness, page 315.

stories; there were no written records. Stories are a medium for conveying wisdom and legacies. It is easy to remember stories because they foster relational connections and create vivid images of people, action, and possibilities.

A story...
• Allows listeners and storytellers to share experiences. • Is a whole experience – feelings, events, characters, etc. – and reveals more about the teller than a list of facts could. • Describes the context of the situation. • Provides details that make the story and lesson memorable.

In summary, the building blocks of Healing Conversations are appreciative, energizing questions and stories. Engaging in inquiry through questions clearly announces that the listener wants to hear and understand the teller. Storytellers relax and begin to feel safe and valued; they tend to reflect, share more, and censor less.

Storytelling is an ancient form of relating and sharing life and history. Story sharing invites relationship. Listeners often shape the stories simply by their presence. Tellers hear their own stories differently in the presence of another. Together, conversation partners create a shared picture of the world while building their relationship.

Chapter 9

THE 1, 2, 3's OF HEALING CONVERSATIONS: INTENTION, PRESENCE, AND CONNECTED LISTENING

Asking appreciative questions and hearing story responses make for lively conversations. However, when listeners hold the intention to connect and enhance the relationship, are fully present, and listen with curiosity and compassion, they amplify the healing potential of these conversations. The 1, 2, 3's are conditions that magnify the power to connect people and create more satisfying and meaningful relationships. These elements, intention, presence, and connected listening, are essential whether the conversation is planned or spontaneous.

NO. 1: BE INTENTIONAL ABOUT YOUR DESIRE TO ENHANCE RELATIONSHIPS

The main purpose of Healing Conversations is to heal the disease of isolation and separation and to build more satisfying relationships. This intention informs our choice of questions and determines the tone of the responses we make to storytellers. If listeners find it challenging to stay on course, remembering the purpose of the conversation will refocus them.

These conversations are dynamic, and the unexpected often crops up. Some memories evoke emotional responses that can trigger and challenge those involved. A clear intention to put relationship building first guides listeners' choice of questions and responses to storytellers.

Before listeners ask questions or make responses they can be sure they are on target if they stop, step back, and ask: Will the question I ask, or statement I make, enhance and support the relationship? If so, do it. If what you anticipate doing will veer off course or is likely to create distance, don't do it.

For example, if the storyteller says something that makes us angry, we have a choice. Do we share our anger or do we ask more questions in order to understand the other's point of view better? If the priority is the relationship, we must put our anger aside, no matter how difficult. Instead, ask questions that help us understand the storyteller's perspective. We might respond, "Tell me more about that," rather than sharing our own angry feelings.

Intention keeps us on track, focused, and on purpose. We can use it to direct our thoughts and responses. When listeners are clear about their purpose, they can make choices about questions and responses, and they usually have more satisfying conversations.

Aunts' Story: Intention Focuses Attention and Guides Actions (Told by Joan.)

I learned a lesson on one visit with my aunts. I was usually totally engaged in their stories and looked forward to them. It was quite easy to be present with them. On one visit, however, I was concerned about some other family drama and was distracted. I had not reminded myself of my intention to be present and build the relationship. Suddenly the stories were not so engaging, and I wondered what had been so fascinating about them in the past.

As soon as I refocused on my purpose for being with my aunts, I became present and immediately heard their stories as I remembered them – interesting, engaging, and often humorous.

It is not what happens out in the world that impacts us. It is our interpretation of those events that shapes our experience. When we bring a clear intention to connect, we will hear elders' stories through that filter. We will notice points of commonality.

———————

Listeners' clear purpose and intention helps them to choose behavior and responses that put the relationship first; it supports the possibility of a greater, more satisfying connection. However, relationship requires two or more people. The elder or dying person will choose how to respond. All endings are not the ideal. We initiate conversations with clarity of purpose, and then let go of the results.

Intention is a
• Clear statement of purpose, desire, and commitment. • Guide for making decisions and choosing actions.

NO. 2: BE PRESENT, MINDFUL, NONJUDGMENTAL, AND STEP OUT OF THE STORYTELLER'S WAY

Presence is a state of being. When we're present, we're 100 percent available, *here and now*. It is the opposite of multitasking. It means having a singular focus on the present moment and person. The person offering a listening presence creates a time apart – dedicated to connecting through inquiry, story-telling, connected listening, and/or silence.

Listening with curiosity and appreciating the other's stories and wisdom are characteristics of presence. It is the greatest and simplest gift of awareness and empathy. Presence amplifies our ability to see and hear beyond the surface. We have access to our intuition, and we are more keenly aware than usual. Our hearts open, and we are more capable of accepting the other unconditionally.

Stepping out of storytellers' way is akin to letting them take the lead. The conversation is all about them. The intention is to know the *storyteller*, to grow closer, and to help *the loved one* find peace and acceptance. While the focus is on the story-teller, listeners report that they benefit from engaging in Healing Conversations as much as elders. Even as the focus is on elders, listeners learn about themselves. When they are present and open their hearts, they relax and increase their capacity to connect. Giving and receiving are part of a sharing cycle.

Engagement isn't always verbal; it may mean sitting togeth-er without words. Silence is a gift, and the listener who is comfortable with it gives a lot. When listeners are comfortable, peaceful, and have an intention to connect, the engagement is likely to be satisfying for both, even without any words. Many report that the silent presence of another makes a difference – some feel comforted just knowing they are not alone.

When we are present with another,
• Our full attention is on the person and conversation, distractions disappear.
• We are totally in this moment – past and future slip away.
• We are curious and open to learning.
• We experience a certain degree of calm, even as we are at a somewhat heightened state of awareness or consciousness.
• We are aware that being engaged may mean sitting together without words.

A hospice volunteer shares his experience of a conversation that made a difference although it was conducted in silence. He was present and listened to his intuition.

Jack's Story: Profound Silent Conversation

I was part of a hospice emergency response team that went into situations when death was near and there was no family or friends. The person was alone. One Christmas Eve, I was called into a nursing home to be with Rosemary. When I arrived at the home, I asked where I'd find her, and the nurse answered, "We've put her down at the end of the hall in a room by herself. We had to isolate her from other patients because her constant and loud moaning disturbed everyone."

I found Rosemary by following the moaning. She was

propped in a sitting position as a way to ease her pain. She had no ability to talk.

When I saw the look on her face, I wanted to run but forced myself to go closer. As I came nearer to the bed, she moaned more loudly. I didn't know what to do and just wanted out of there. So I left and went to the nursing station. Usually they have a book with notes about each patient: their likes, their family, and what comforted them. I hoped to find something to guide me. There were no notes on Rosemary.

I forced myself to go back into her room. Searching for some clue about what to do, my eyes fell on a book. "Good, I can read to her. I know how to do that. Maybe it will calm her," I assured myself as I began reading. The moaning continued.

Finally, I stopped reading because it was too much of a struggle to compete with the moaning. I sat back, took a deep breath, went into my heart, and asked myself, "What would I want if I were in this situation?" The answer came in a flash.

I broke all of the rules. I sat on the bed where I could look her in the eyes, and took both of her hands in mine. We just sat like that for a long time. I told her, "I'm going to be here with you. If you need to cry, cry. Do what you need to do. I'll be here." The moaning continued for a while and then got quieter and quieter. Finally, she became quiet, too.

If I moved my hand, she'd reach for it. She'd pull me back closer to her. After about half an hour, she smiled at me. We sat in silent connection, eyes on one another for a long time. She became more and more peaceful, and finally she took her last breath – in peace.

When Jack stopped, took a breath, and became present, his intuition told him exactly what Rosemary needed. He had the courage to listen to his own inner wisdom. Doing so made the difference between a miserable death and a good one for Rosemary.

Being present means the listener is calm, focused, and remembers the purpose of the conversation. When listeners are attentive to storytellers in this way, they hear with their hearts *and* ears. They have access to their intuition, which gives guidance about the needs and wants of the storyteller. As listeners tune in to their conversation partners, they might silently ask themselves: What will enhance the connection? What does the storyteller need now? Answers are likely to come to mind as listeners are quiet and listen for inner wisdom.

As the listener is present, nonjudgmental, and focused on the relationship a magnetic pull develops between listener and storyteller. The loved one feels it and gravitates into the reassuring embrace of the conversation. The partners' ability to hear and connect is heightened. Both feel enriched.

NO. 3: BE A CONNECTED LISTENER: LISTENING WITH REVERENCE

Listening in Healing Conversations differs from most daily interactions. It goes beyond the skills of active listening, which can be applied mechanically. In Healing Conversations listeners' first priority is to bond with loved ones. They provide support so storytellers can comfortably share and reflect upon their experience.

Connected listeners are curious and expect to learn something new. They use the skills of active listening from a caring and loving place. They are nonjudgmental and accepting. This quality of listening creates a web of connections built upon trust.

These conversations are not designed as an opportunity for listeners to express their own feelings, their thoughts, or to give advice. They aren't a time for listeners to get hurts off their chests. Being the listener in Healing Conversations requires putting aside your own reactions and feelings – for the moment. In his best selling book, *Seven Habits of Highly Effective People*, Stephen Covey suggests, listen first to understand before speaking. That advice applies to connected listening. The focus is on the elder or person dying, and the goal is to enhance connections with them. Listening to understand makes that happen.

Jean's story illustrates the kind of understanding, acceptance, and change possible when people engage in Healing Conversations:

Jean's Story:
Understanding and Acceptance At Last

In the last couple of months of my mother's life, I stayed with her on weekends in her apartment. She and I had had a rocky relationship – probably more on my side than on hers. Probably the issues stemmed from the fact that I was so much like her. As we spent more time together, the distance started to fade.

My father died twenty years earlier than my mother; I was in my late twenty's at that time. When I was five, he was in an accident. My early recollections are of him at home in a hospital bed after the accident getting physical therapy, then being on crutches. He became a different person after that accident.

He'd been a successful entrepreneur and a community leader, but after the accident, he wasn't even able to dress himself without help. Eventually, he had to sell his businesses and create a much lesser job for himself. He persevered despite being in constant pain. That determination took its toll; he was not pleasant to live with.

I was involved in everything at school. It was only when I was older that I realized I had done that so I wouldn't have to be at home much. My father was a really tough person to be around. My two brothers and I often talked about not being able to understand why Mom stayed with him. We sometimes wondered if she just wasn't strong enough to stand up to him or leave.

I'd spent my entire life thinking, "Why is she doing this?" Yet I never dared to broach that subject until one of our weekends together. I sensed that she was open to that question, so I finally asked, "Why did you put up with the way Dad treated you?"

Her response surprised me. "He was the love of my life," she said. "Your father was the most fun, the most easy-going man I'd ever known. His was the first name on the guest list whenever anyone planned a party. After the accident, he was a different person." Those images and memories of him, as he was before the accident, were what she carried. I realized in that moment how these memories had helped her deal with a situation she simply accepted as the hand they had been dealt.

Hearing the love and commitment she had for the man who lived inside the man we knew, was a revelation to me. It was the first time she and I had talked as adult women about an experience we shared but saw so differently – she as a wife and mother, I as a child. I finally understood that she had been waiting for me to grow up enough to be able to hear the truth with compassion – for him – not for her.

This conversation helped me to realize the role she had played. She navigated the perilous waters between his pain and disappointment and her need to protect us from him. We never saw that because it was all done behind the scenes. She tried to influence him to be a better father without attacking his pride. Finally, I could see her strength and knew that it was she who held the family together.

She died a couple of months after this conversation. I was fortunate to be with her constantly through the final weeks of her life.

Loads of people showed up at her funeral. Many of them said to me, "You ARE your mother — you look like her, you sound like her, you have her sense of humor."

This was the first time in my life I would honestly say, "That is the greatest compliment you could give me." Our revealing conversation had opened a whole world to us.

Jean's story illuminates the possibility for the unexpected when we ask questions, are present, and ready to hear a different version of the story. Listening with compassion and without judgment cues the storyteller. Jean believes her mother waited for her to mature before talking about their lives and the man in them. She wanted Jean to be mature enough to hear with an open heart and mind.

—————

The next story illustrates the possibilities when listeners attend to the elder and are able to listen for the meaning beyond the words.

Roz's Story: She Heard the Real Question

I remember a conversation with my father just days before his small-cell lung cancer spread to his brain. We were driving when he asked me, "Why does everyone love your mother so much?" I started to say why, then stopped. I realized that what he asked was not the real question. He was asking if *he* was loved, so I shifted my response. I simply said, "I love you," and shared why. The smile on his face told me I had heard his real concern. We had quite an intimate moment between us.

It is a precious gift to be loved, to be heard, and to be acknowledged. Roz demonstrated compassionate listening. She gave her dad a gift, and his smile and connection was one to her in return. Listening and trusting what she heard between the lines allowed Roz and her dad to have an especially loving and intimate moment.

Connected listeners go beyond active listening skills, they:

- Remember that their first priority is connecting and enhancing relationship.
- Focus on the storyteller rather than their own experience.
- Allow the storyteller time to think in silence.
- Encourage storytellers' emotions and disclosures.
- Keep eye contact.
- Take a moment of silent reflection before responding; take a breath after the speaker finishes so each person has time to reflect on what was shared.

BEING HEARD: ANOTHER SIDE OF LISTENING

The basic human need to be heard and accepted is a foundational concept of Healing Conversations. "You hear me into being," Katherine's friend, Sally, told her. She listens to this friend with care, respect, and acceptance in a way that no one else does. She reflects understanding and adds value by giving a more global and meaningful perspective. Her questions announce to her friend, "I hear and understand you."

Being heard by another helps us to hear ourselves better. When we speak of our experiences, feelings, and events, and when another hears us, we understand them and ourselves more fully. The presence of the witness is an essential dimension to the storyteller's self-understanding. Storytellers gain a degree of clarity they couldn't find if they were trying to understand by talking only to themselves, inside their heads.

The following story is about Katherine, who needed to hear her own inner wisdom in order to make a life-or-death decision. She was able to do so only after two others had heard her.

Katherine's Story:
He Listened to Me and I Heard Myself

It felt like taking Mom off life support was the same as killing her. I was so torn about what to do. It was the week after Christmas, and my mother had been moved from the assisted living facility to the hospital. She was seriously ill, and the medical staff was gently pushing me toward taking her off life support.

My brain knew one thing, but my heart was struggling. Knowing the facts of her condition, you wouldn't think this would be a tough decision, but I was searching for a *soul* decision. Although my mother had originally executed directives that there be no extraordinary means, a couple of days before re-entering the hospital she had revoked them all. She made it clear that she had no intention of dying; she wanted to live.

This night was particularly miserable. I was sitting alone with her, holding her hand on this blowy, blizzardy night, just waiting for something or someone to tell me what to do. The Intensive Care Unit was dark. The only sounds were the ventilator and the beep of her heart monitor.

I called Maureen, the nurse who'd been with Mom at her assisted living facility, and told her that Mom had revoked the directives. She said, "I think that was fear talking." That conversation was helpful but didn't get me to a decision.

Later, I was still sitting holding Mom's hand and was no closer to an answer than before, when a minister I'd never seen before stopped in the doorway. He hesitated and looked at me for a moment before taking a step in. He said, "It looks like you could use some company," and he sat down on the far side of Mom's bed.

This was my night in Gethsemane; I was in deep, deep pain about what to do. This man entered the room with a deep sense of compassion and no agenda. It was all done in kindness. I replied, "Yes, I can." I told him about my mother, her life of adventure and her change of mind about the advance directives. "She's always been feisty, and it isn't totally out of character for her to revoke the directives; it's somewhat in character."

He listened and all he said was, "You know we will all die at some point. Tell me, how would your mother want to die?"

The minute he asked that question I knew the answer in my heart. It was suddenly clear: "She'd want me with her," I replied. I also knew that the only way I could be sure I'd be with her was to make this decision. I couldn't live in the hospital for however long death might take if she remained on life support. I wanted to be with her at that moment.

Once I got that clarity, I knew I needed to be there, and that meant disconnecting life support. I also realized that she was frightened and needed the family and a minister there. We got those people in the room, and we allowed my mom to die peacefully.

That minister just listened and that was it. I'll be forever grateful that he took the risk of coming into the room and sitting with me. I needed someone to hear me. I needed to talk to someone so that I could hear my own inner wisdom.

This story illustrates the simple yet profound effects of listening. We don't need to solve other people's problems. However, if we listen and ask thoughtful questions we help them to think through the options and make the best decision for themselves.

———◆———

Three elements are essential to Healing Conversations: intention, presence and connected listening. When these attributes are coupled with appreciative questions and storytelling, hearts open and relationships shift.

Chapter 10

PREPARING FOR HEALING CONVERSATIONS: LITTLE THINGS MAKE A DIFFERENCE

Healing Conversations invite intimacy beyond the usual conversational fare. Creating an inviting and comfortable environment nurtures the conversation. Environmental variables can make all the difference. Attending to logistical factors such as timing, length of conversation, where, and who is present, sets the stage for a more fruitful conversation. A safe and inviting environment supports the kind of interaction associated with Healing Conversations.

Timing is important. Mariam, a friend who does life-interviews for a living, discovered how true that statement is.

Mariam's Story: When? Why Not Now?

One evening I invited my mother and father to dinner. My two grown children also ate with us. As we sat around the kitchen table, Dad spontaneously began telling stories.

Thank heavens I remembered my tape recorder and jumped up to get it while trying not to interrupt Dad's flow. It recorded his stories as well as requests to pass the potatoes and lapses of time when he'd stop to take a mouthful of food. It also captured many rich experiences. Sometimes I'd ask a question, but mostly we listened. Hearing that tape in Dad's own voice is a gift. I gave copies to my many siblings and know their offspring will continue to appreciate them for generations to come.

However, a few months later, Dad was diagnosed with cancer. I asked him for more stories, but the opportunity was gone. Although he had been a natural storyteller, he no longer had the energy or concentration needed to share. The window of opportunity was shut. Since then, I've encouraged people to ask for stories now.

Mariam's reminder was a factor in choosing the title for this book. If we don't engage in these kinds of interactions now we may miss the chance. We can't predict the future or how long the window of opportunity will remain open.

———◈◈◈———

Tony writes about the changes that occurred in his mom. As her illness progressed, Tony had to work around her health and level of coherence.

> It was a weird time. Toward the end, Mom began to get dementia and had good days and bad. I had to get stories when she was coherent enough to tell them. There was no time to waste. I got to know her better only as she was drifting away.

> I am so thankful that we engaged in these Healing Conversations when we did. Instead of the usual progression of her disease, Mom died suddenly in 2005 when she fell and hit her head. I am glad that she went quickly rather than after dementia stole her away slowly. Yet I am sad that my children never got to know her. I miss her.

The lesson from these stories and those told by so many others is that the sooner we begin these conversations the better. We just don't know how long we can wait and still hear the important stories. It is a luxury to have years to engage in these conversations.

If we want to know our loved ones better, enhance and mend relationships, it's important to make the decision and act on it, now. Having years to develop these conversations provides lots of opportunity for surprises. It also creates a foundation upon which to have the difficult discussions needed toward the end of life. It is easy to delay the start of these meaningful conversations. However, even if we don't begin until the storyteller has received a terminal diagnosis, the process will be rewarding.

The Invitation

Listeners often speak of their hesitation to initiate these more intimate conversations. They want to have them, but wonder about the elder's reaction. The more comfortable and confident you are when you make the invitation, the more likely you'll find the same in return. Remember you are giving your loved one the gift of your attention and appreciation. It is a rare experience to have someone truly listen without judgment. Loved ones are most likely to accept your invitation with gratitude, once they understand what you're offering.

Most people love sharing their stories once they begin. Some will need you to make them comfortable before participating. Some people may initially profess they have nothing interesting to share; some have trouble believing any one wants to hear about their lives. If you tailor the invitation to the individual, if you are genuinely curious, and if you are willing to listen compassionately, you are likely to get a positive response, even if it is a hesitant one at first.

An invitation might be as straightforward as: "I've heard you talk about playing soccer when you were young. Is there a particular game or experience that stands out for you? Or you might begin with a more open invitation such as: Would you tell me stories about your life? What was it like growing up? What stories stand out for you?"

Once the person agrees to participate, it is time to address logistics: when to have the conversation, the length, who is to be present, permission to say, "I prefer not to talk about that," and the option for recording.

Time: Length of Conversation

Conversations have a rhythm and timing of their own, and we can be in sync if we tune in to those natural signals. Conversations begin, energy builds to a crescendo, and then wanes. Pay attention to the story and the storyteller. People may only have the energy to answer one question at a time and may take minutes to complete the story.

Some storytellers need silent time before or after speaking. It isn't that they don't want to share, but their quiet indicates their thinking style. They may be reflective thinkers and need time to ponder before speaking. Give them time in silence.

On the other hand, some people need to talk so they can clarify their thinking. They may respond with all kinds of information that seems irrelevant, rambling, or off-topic. These people need time to verbalize and hear themselves. Talking is their editing process and helps them define the point they want to make. Building connections cannot be rushed.

Place: Quiet, Private, and Comfortable

The environment can support and encourage the conversation or make it more difficult. Think about the difference between having a private conversation in a noisy restaurant with people nearby or in a private and quiet place, possibly in nature, where it is easy to hear and see each other. With age, background noise may make it difficult to hear those near us. Be aware of the environment because it can nurture conversations or make it more difficult to share personal information and stories.

The best environment is one that is comfortable and natural for the storyteller. Many conversations happen at the table or in a comfortable living room. Sometimes the person is confined to bed, so that is where conversations occur. Walking together or traveling in a car is another possibility. Many topics have been discussed while sharing "windshield" time.

It is not always possible to choose the environment. If that is the case, be aware of what is available and do what you can to make the setting as comfortable, inviting, and private as possible. When people feel safe and comfortable, trust increases, and connecting is easier. A nurturing environment invites both parties to be more present and to share more of themselves.

Who Is Present?
Advantages of One on One or a Group

Usually Healing Conversations take place in private between two people. Some people are more likely to share personally and reflect in a meaningful way if they are alone with a listener. That situation gives some conversation partners a sense of intimacy and feels safe.

However, some people enjoy sharing their stories with several family members at the same time. This is a different experience. Others in the room may add to the conversation by asking questions. They might tell a story about the elder and his or her effect on them that prompts more reminiscences. Sharing with a group energizes some storytellers; the more people the more animated they are.

A Hospice Family's Story:
Last Healing Conversation (Told by Joan)

As a hospice volunteer, I sit vigil with people who are actively dying; sometimes their families are present. One family was particularly distraught. Their beloved grandmother, Gracie, was on the bed actively dying. The adult granddaughter and grandson walked into the room. The granddaughter was beside herself with grief and crumpled into a ball in the chair beside her grandmother's bed. She wept. Her brother tried to comfort her while he grieved his own impending loss.

As we sat around the grandmother's bed, I asked, "What

are some special times you shared with Gracie?"

They readily entered into storytelling. We laughed and cried together as stories allowed them to relive precious times with Gracie. What one didn't think of, the other added. They reminded each other of long rides in the car with both grandparents, and the picnics their grandmother packed. At one point, the granddaughter spoke of something she and her grandmother had done; the mother looked shocked. Across the bed, the granddaughter asked her mother, "You never knew that did you, Mom? Grams could keep a secret." We all smiled.

They told tales of the grandmother's intuition. "Remember that Thanksgiving when Grams said, 'There's an invisible dinner guest?' Suzie hadn't told anyone she was pregnant, but now it wasn't a secret anymore." Each family member added new details and different stories.

The mother looked at me and said, "Gracie wasn't seen as the smart one in her family."

I replied, "Maybe not but she sure knew a lot about loving and being a terrific mother and grandmother." They all agreed. It was a time of honoring this caring woman.

In this case, the family told stories. We are told that hearing is the last sense to go. I imagine that grandmother, Gracie, felt loved as her family honored her and spoke of her so lovingly. At the end of the evening, Gracie simply sighed. It was her last breath.

In this situation, the whole family gathered together and honored their grandmother in a way that one person couldn't do. The interaction among them added joy. The spirit of the whole family's love filled the room. Sometimes the situation dictates who is present and who becomes the storyteller.

———◆———

Whatever the situation you can probably turn most environments into engaging ones even if they don't match your picture of how the conversation should look.

Environmental Elements

Below are some typical environmental elements to consider:

- **Physical comfort:** Ask what would make the loved one most comfortable – a drink, different position, or a different place?

- **Temperature:** Is the room the right temperature? Does the elder need air, a shawl, or a sweater?

- **Time:** What is the best time of day to talk? People have schedules and also natural rhythms that make them more available mentally and physically at certain times and not at others. For example, naptime will not be as productive as some other time.

- **Privacy:** Ask if this is an opportune time and place. If the loved one is in an institution, professional caregivers are likely to interrupt. You might assure the elder that you can stop and pick up the conversation when the caregiver leaves.

- **Confidentiality:** Since a sense of safety leads to more fulfilling conversations, it is important for the storyteller to know what will happen to their precious and often private life stories. Once they know who will hear this material, and how it will be used, they may relax. It is wise to ask if the storyteller is willing for you to share their material in the ways you want.

Recording

Too often we have marvelous conversations and afterward wish we had captured that interaction in some way, but it is too late. Part of preparing for Healing Conversations includes decisions about preserving them.

Some questions about recording are:

- Do you record the conversation, or take notes? If you take notes, do you do it during or after the conversation?

- If you use a recording device, which one: audio or video?

- Do you ask permission, or tell them that you are recording and why?

Digital audio recorders are unobtrusive. Many include software to transfer digital audio files to your computer and can translate from audio to written format. Small flash video cameras are available. They are relatively inexpensive, and easy to use.

If you do record, be sure to do an equipment check prior to the conversation. We can tell you from personal experience that realizing you didn't get a fantastic story recorded – one you thought you were capturing – is a real disappointment and a lost opportunity that cannot be replicated.

Recording may impact the conversation. Storytellers often initially protest that they don't want to be recorded but once the conversation begins they usually forget the recorder. If they are hesitant, tell them why it is important to have a record of the conversation. Let them know who will have access to the information. Some elders feel honored when you value their stories enough to keep them as a legacy.

The purpose of the conversation impacts decisions about recording. If legacy is important, some form of recording is necessary. However, if conversations are primarily about healing and building relationship, recording is not necessary. Hearing a story in the person's own voice is priceless. After the elder is gone many people wish that they had a recording of the voice and stories.

The next story illustrates the concern and possible reactions of recording and sharing others' life stories.

Joan's story:
Let Me Tell You More If Its Going to Be Published

After particularly touching or funny conversations with my aunts, I made notes. They were the foundation for a journal article and a newspaper feature. My aunts knew I was writing about them, but they didn't read the notes or the material prior to publication. When the material was published, I became concerned about their reactions. Would they find the portraits unattractive, unflattering, or distasteful? Would they stop having these conversations? Would they be more circumspect in what they shared?

On the next visit, while sitting around the table I brought out the newspaper clipping and published article with trepidation. What would they say? They were both very private people who didn't share much about themselves with outsiders. In fact, Eva had refused to be the subject of a newspaper article for her beloved geriatrician; what would she think? I feared that the room would suddenly acquire an icy chill when I showed them the newspaper and journal articles.

Their reactions were a delightful surprise. After hearing what was written they both rushed to talk at once – a new behavior. They wanted to tell new stories. Nettie became even more animated than usual and stood up to demonstrate the point of one of her jokes. After that they'd say,

"This is one for your book." Both were proud to be memorialized in such a public way.

While my aunts' reactions are not the ones everyone will have, they remind us of how much people want to be recognized in some way – even very private people. It also reminds us to check our assumptions. The reaction you get may be the opposite of what you expect.

—————

Enriching conversations can take place anywhere. Yet creating an inviting, comfortable, and safe environment nurtures those involved. Doing so invites the conversation partners to focus on the stories and relationship rather than on distracting environmental factors.

Recording is important to consider while preparing. Decide the purpose of the recording and how you would use it. Recorded material is likely to be valued by generations to come. One factor to consider is that the best conversations are often spontaneous, and it is only after the fact that you realize how much you'd like to have that experience recorded. The solution is to make a habit of recording.

Chapter 11

DEALING WITH
UNEXPECTED AND
DIFFICULT CIRCUMSTANCES

People's lives and experiences aren't neatly wrapped in pretty boxes. Elders and the dying may carry long-term hurts, resentments, and disappointments that make them irritable or just difficult. They may be mourning the loss of so much and not be in a particularly sharing mode. They may not have spent much time in reflection and may not be sure what to say.

Healing Conversations invite elders to explore topics that require them to reflect on their feelings and beliefs. When listeners pay attention and put their judgments aside, they set the stage so that storytellers can share the more intimate details of their lives. When they do decide to share, be prepared for the unexpected.

Sometimes storytellers will even surprise themselves with what comes out of their mouths. Even the most prepared listeners may find themselves caught off guard, especially when relating to people they love. Old and deeply entrenched family dynamics may be activated. Therefore, listeners need to be prepared to deal with their own and others' reactions, suddenly revealed secrets, difficult and silent people, and strained relationships.

DEALING WITH SURPRISES, FEELINGS, AND AWKWARD MOMENTS

Healing Conversations create a safe environment that encourages elders and the dying to speak without censoring. As they recognize that they won't be judged, they may allow secrets and feelings to be expressed that they've held inside for years or decades.

Sometimes storytellers reveal something that is quite unexpected, and the information stops listeners in their tracks. What do listeners do when they're caught off guard and their own strong feelings come to the surface? A few stories illustrate what some empathic listeners have done.

Pam's Story: Focus on Intention: Hold the Hurt

My mother was telling me the story of the family reunion celebrating her seventieth birthday. She said it was one of the most meaningful and valuable highlights of her life. As she enthusiastically told her story, I realized that I had not been invited, and felt hurt listening to Mom speaking about this "special" event in her life. It was not part of my family experience. I had to deal with two simultaneous conversations occurring in my head.

One stream focused on my hurt. "This so-called 'family' reunion might have been wonderful for her, but what about me? How is she defining family if I wasn't included? I didn't even know it occurred."

The second inner conversation confronted me with the fact that Mom was dying, and I was here to be with her. I was hurting, but decided to "Shush!" the part of me that wanted to remind her that I was neither there nor invited.

After I had time to think, I was so glad that during the conversation I just remained curious about her birthday party and didn't confront her. Upon reflection, I remembered what I had told my parents: "I can't see you until you've stopped drinking." When Mom turned 70 she was still drinking. I had cut myself off from them at the time.

In Pam's case, her clarity about the purpose of her visit allowed her to put aside her own immediate reactions of hurt and abandonment. She took a moment and made a decision. She'd focus on her mother's excitement about the party and what it had meant to her, rather than bring her own hurt feelings into the conversation. Doing so gave her time to put the situation into context.

The next story demonstrates commitment to the relationship. By finding the strength to search for positive qualities about a difficult mother, Kathleen discovered a precious exchange with her mother.

Kathleen's Story: The Choice

In the days before my mother's death, this woman who had always frightened me became very frail and terrified. In one conversation, my mother was sad because she didn't have many friends. "I don't understand why I never had any friends," she sighed.

I tried to think quickly and asked myself, "What can I say that isn't a lie?" It would have been easy to tell her what I'd observed and the many behaviors that repelled people. Instead, I willed myself to go to a place in my heart that remembered the beauty of her, the many wonderful parts of her. In that moment, that was all there was.

"They don't know what they missed," I replied. I wasn't just being nice. I felt sad that no one else saw those valued parts of her. I cried as Mom laid her head on my shoulder. My tears were for both of us. It was about lost opportunity. I felt sad for her and for us. We had missed so much.

This conversation was the closest I'd ever felt to Mom. It came as a total surprise. I felt so blessed that we had that time together, and that at least one of her burdens was lifted. She knew that I loved her and saw some of her better qualities — ones that others had missed. The conversation was especially important because she died the next day.

These listeners had to deal with their own emotional responses while remaining present to their loved ones. They chose to go to their hearts and enhance the relationship rather than bring negative issues into the conversation. Some might argue that this wasn't honest. We'd say it was definitely honest; it just didn't include the negative comments. The listeners made a choice that was aligned with their commitment to enhance the relationship. Intention trumped the possibility of confrontation.

<hr />

Even some professional caregivers have told us they want to run from the room when elders become emotional. Some say they avoid the person, if possible. They don't know what to do or say. It is not always easy to deal with emotions, expressed or felt, or to respond to surprises while continuing to listen to another. These moments can be awkward. A few suggestions for dealing with some of these difficult situations are:

> **Do nothing:** Take a deep breath or two. Quiet your mind, find your composure, and be ready to be present to the other. It is easy to get lost in your own reactions and lose focus on your goals. A few seconds of breathing gives you time to remember your desire to enhance the relationship and get back on track.

Talk to yourself: Remember why you are there: to gain a deeper understanding of the storyteller, and to give them the experience of being seen and heard. Listening in this way, you will learn how they experience and understand their lives and the world.

Allow storytellers to express their feelings: Be ready to honor emotions. You don't need to soothe or stop them. You are not there to fix anything. Feelings are part of the process. Your acceptance of this expression will allow it to happen. Dealing with feelings in this way is truly a gift for all. Simply sit quietly and breathe. Listeners' comfort gives storytellers the message that they are safe expressing emotions.

Stay in your adult: These conversations require an adult perspective, which means putting the other and the relationship first. Listeners' emotions interfere with the ability to be nonjudgmental. When something difficult comes up, let go of defensiveness, the desire to explain, or even the urge to express deep hurt – at least for the moment. You can rethink the situation when you are by yourself.

After you have built a foundation for this new level of intimacy, you might then discuss your feelings with your conversation partner. In Healing Conversations, the focus is on the storyteller and not the listener's reactions. Any response needs to be thoughtful and one that ensures the conversation enhances the relationship.

RELUCTANT STORYTELLERS

For any number of reasons, people may not respond immediately to the listener's request for stories. Some people are not in the habit of reflecting or putting their thoughts into words. They may prefer action to talk. The request may ask storytellers to reflect in ways that aren't usual for them. They may not think in terms of stories. They may think they have little of interest to share.

May's Story: The Value of the Ordinary

May wanted to know more about her Uncle Lester. He hadn't had a spectacular career or done anything newsworthy, but she loved and appreciated him. She asked if he'd allow her to inquire about his life.

Lester clearly stated, "I don't have any stories worth sharing. My life was quite ordinary."

Her response was enthusiastic and brilliant: "Good! That is just what I want to hear – your life in the insignificant and ordinary times. Those are what make us who we are." He slowly began relating events in his life, all the while assuring her they weren't important. She learned about his love of gardening and the prize rose he grew. She was surprised to find they had this interest in common. She learned how he met and married her aunt. The list went on and on.

May's statement that her uncle's everyday life was what she wanted to hear reassured him. Sometimes we have to be quick on our feet to tease out stories and help the potential story-teller recognize we're not asking for fully formed memoirs about exciting life events and heroics. Be patient and clear. The message you are sending is that you want to know the person better and are curious about his or her life.

SILENT ELDERS

Some elders, especially if they are quite ill or nearing death, may be silent, and the thought of engaging them in conversation seems daunting. In fact, it is even difficult to know if the listener's presence makes a difference. In those times, listeners need to remind themselves that a listening presence is valuable no matter appearances. Conversations can be wordless. Listeners need to trust this process even if there is no evidence that anything is happening.

Alan describes himself: "I'm a talker and usually don't listen well. I like to talk. I was assigned to work with a silent client. This hospice assignment challenged me.

Alan's Story: Conversation with No Words

This hospice patient, Mark, gave me plenty of listening practice. I forced myself to listen to all of his movements and anything he said. Mostly, I had to listen to my own thoughts.

Mark was a retired Marine sergeant. Although he seldom spoke, when he did, he was gruff. The household was chaotic and noisy. There was a lot of arguing between him and his care-giving wife. He criticized her constantly, and she shot back in-kind comments.

He didn't talk to me at all and didn't want to answer questions. His wife would leave for respite as I sat beside his bed three days a week – up to ten hours a week – in complete silence. After three months, Mark finally said, "Hi, Alan," when I walked in. I celebrated inside myself and thought we must have made some kind of connection.

No meaningful conversation ever materialized. Instead, I sat by as Mark watched loud and often violent TV programs, ones I would never watch at home. I tried to block out the disturbing noise. However, I was vigilant and persistent as I sat with Mark over many months.

The high point of the relationship was one day late in our time together. I spoke to him before leaving and said my usual, "Goodbye, Mark."

This time Mark replied, "'Bye, Alan. Thank you." I was moved to tears by these four words. I sat in my car reflecting on what I might have added to this man's life by listening to his loud silence. I would never know.

Alan persevered although he received almost no signals that assured him that his presence mattered. He had to trust that he was helpful. The situation may test our willingness and resolve to be a silent presence.

———⊸•⊶———

Silent people or those who give little response can be a challenge. Listeners must be confident of the value of their listening presence even in the absence of words. These situations call on our ability to be still and calm. When we are quiet, we can pick up on subtle, nonverbal cues. We have to learn to trust our inner voice and believe our presence makes a difference even if never acknowledged.

ELDERS' SECRETS

People keep secrets for a variety of reasons. They may believe that the information is too private to share. They may be embarrassed or ashamed when they think of the story. They may be judging themselves so harshly they cannot imagine anyone else's acceptance. Some people are unwilling to revisit some situation because doing so is too painful. No matter why people keep them, secrets separate the person holding them from others. Sharing them often brings relief to the person and creates a bond between the teller and listener.

Sometimes elders just can't hold their lifelong secrets any longer. They know time is limited, and they want to be released from their shame, guilt, or pain. The initial reason for withholding information may no longer be valid. Although we don't know for sure what motivates someone to share a long-held secret, many are able to let go of pain and anguish when they do.

Leticia's Story: Finally Unburdening Herself

My ninety-three-year-old mother's invitation for me to visit had urgency about it. When I arrived she felt compelled to tell me her story immediately. "I've got something I want to tell you," she blurted out. I understood her intensity when she revealed the secret she had carried for so many years.

She told me this story: "When I was twelve, everyone in the family went out one evening except me and my eighteen-year-old brother. I was comfortable staying home and I soon went to bed and quickly fell asleep. Suddenly, my eyes snapped open. My brother was in my bed and on top of me. He was trying to rape me, but I screamed and cried and kept hitting him. Finally, he got scared and ran." "I've never told anyone, even my best friend, and I've told her everything – except this. I kept this secret."

My mother then explained that from that time on she was afraid of men and kept them at a distance. She married very late in life for her time. I remember, after my father died, there was a wonderful neighbor who helped us a lot and wanted to spend time with my mother, but she continued to shoo him away. Now I understand. Her secret explains a lot. I respect her more for having lived with this secret for so long, and for having finally released the burden to me.

Leticia responded to the urgency in her mother's voice. By listening, she allowed her mother to release a burden she'd carried for decades. Obviously, Leticia had a trusting relationship with her mother; it allowed her to finally let go of this old hurt.

———

It takes trust – and maybe desperation – to share long-held secrets. It is a memorable moment when the storyteller feels safe enough to reveal this information. Hopefully, listeners can be present enough to attend to the storyteller rather than to their own reactions. Allow yourself to imagine the feelings of the storyteller, what it has been like to carry this burden alone for all this time. Sit quietly, and allow the revelation to settle into the conversation. Elders are honoring you when they tell their secrets. Your loved one trusts you enough to confide. You might voice your gratitude.

While some feel the need to unburden, others will clutch their secrets to the end. The bits of information that can't be validated or explored can frustrate survivors, especially when the secret haunts the dying one.

Pat's Story: Secrets to the Grave

Pat and her sisters didn't discover family mysteries until after their father died. When they were sorting through family papers, they came upon a name they couldn't identify. Their mother was reluctant to give much information, but finally offhandedly said, "Oh, that was the name of my first husband." End of story! She was not willing to add any more information. The daughters were dumbfounded. They had no idea their mother had been married more than once.

However, more secrets emerged when the daughters discovered a paper marked "legal-marriage." When they asked their mother about it, she told them she'd had two weddings to their father. Their parents had discovered that their first marriage was not legal because it occurred before the required yearlong waiting period after a divorce. The actual legal marriage took place when the oldest daughter was seven months old. After some additional questioning, the mother disclosed that she'd actually met their father while still married to her first husband.

These revelations made the daughters wonder what else they didn't know about their family. Pat gave her mom many opportunities to talk about her past and family, but she never shared anything more. If the daughters didn't discover information on their own, they didn't know it.

Pat feels sad, not so much because she didn't hear the secrets, but because they seemed to haunt her mother. In the last two weeks of her life, guilt tormented Pat's mom. She kept repeating, "I just can't speak the truth." She went to the grave with her secrets and unresolved issues.

Secrets have an effect on the person holding them. They change relationships and shape lives. Yet, people share them only when they feel safe enough to do so. They may have to love and forgive themselves before they are ready.

———◆———

As listeners, we do our best to build trust and a safe environment. We listen without judgment. However, elders may have such strong concerns that no matter what others do, they hold their secrets and accompanying feelings. We do our best but do not have control over the outcomes. Listeners offer their presence; it is the storytellers' choice whether or not to accept.

Each person decides how much to reveal, and how much to share with another. Even if you have co-created a safe environment, the elder or dying person may decide to refrain from sharing. The decision about what to share is not yours. As a conversation partner, you may be curious, but satisfying your curiosity is not the purpose of these conversations. All you can do is offer yourself as a nonjudgmental listener.

STUCK IN REPETITIOUS RUTS

Many elders have certain stories they repeat habitually, like a stuck record. It is frustrating enough if they are positive stories, but much more difficult if they are tales of victimization.[30] We may want to run; we may shut down. It is as if there is a script the teller follows.

Telling your story is important, but getting trapped in repeated and rote tellings of these events is not helpful. These tellers no longer hear themselves, and others don't pay much attention either. Listeners are usually bored and want to escape. Tellers don't receive what they need so long as they are stuck in this loop.

Following is the story of someone who clung to his identity as a victim. Greg seemed stuck and stressed.

Greg's Story: Victim Identity

Greg had a story, and he wanted lots of people to hear it. He told it often. He continued to focus on the characters and the drama of his story. He recounted the litany of slights to him: He had gone out of his way to help David, his brother, who didn't appreciate what he'd done for him. Greg wanted everyone to know how David had mistreated him. No one appreciated his gargantuan effort to give. Laura, the listener, continued to ask, "What are your feelings?" Instead of answering her questions, Greg told more stories about being mistreated. Laura was frustrated and emphatically declared, "I don't want to hear about David. I want to know what about this story is most important to you. How do you feel about David and this situation?"

---

30 If the person was involved in some catastrophic and traumatic event, such as war, terror, or a crime, they may need to talk with an experienced counselor.

With this question, Greg finally stopped, took a deep breath, and his face got red. "David doesn't appreciate me or recognize how I go out of my way for him. I sometimes leave my own family to help him. Worse than not appreciating me, he took advantage of me."

Once Greg acknowledged his feelings, he became clear. He admitted that being helpful is important to him; it is part of his identity. When David didn't acknowledge Greg's generosity, Greg felt worthless. It was Greg who was needy. He sacrificed so that others would recognize and affirm his worth. Laura and Greg explored his feelings and identified alternative behavior that would take him out of the victim role.

Laura asked questions so that Greg could begin to recognize his part in this drama and address his feelings. She asked him to talk about his own feelings rather than what someone else did to him. Recounting another's misdeeds didn't move the conversation forward. She was direct in this request. When he responded, he had taken the first step toward changing his perceptions and his life.

Repeated and rote storytelling doesn't add understanding or acceptance. Each telling reinforces elders' anger, bitterness, and other dark feelings. If storytellers believe no one cares or understands, and they don't know what else to do, they are likely to keep repeating the story. They want to be heard and understood.

Asking storytellers questions about events, feelings, assumptions, and beliefs gives them an opportunity to explore something new. It changes the interaction slightly so that tellers are no longer in rote mode. You may want to try out "The Whole Story" activity described in chapter 3, Acknowledging Multiple Perspectives section. This activity will help the story-teller describe the situation from another's perspective, thus providing clarity, insight, and new understanding.

There is a difference between the repeated telling of a life-less story and the fresh telling of a traumatic one. The latter may be cathartic and healing; sharing the story helps people come to terms with the trauma or unhealed wound. With each telling, the story is likely to become more integrated into the person's life, and the feelings become less intense. Tellers may come to acceptance and forgiveness and eventually come to terms with the situation.

A word of caution: When a terminal patient tells a story of trauma for the first time, it is essential for the listener to be emotionally present. Those near death may need to talk about anger, guilt, or regrets. Allow them to do so. Recognize that people near death may be desperate to let go of some past situation they may have carried for many years. They may need to complete this story in order to find peace.

When the unexpected happens listeners are challenged. They are asked to stay present, not to fix anything. What is helpful is listening without judgment. In Healing Conversations, we can listen and ask probing questions. We can inquire into the story in a way that invites the teller to reflect more on what he or she believes and feels. Questions and willingness to listen are what we need if we are to be supportive. A summary of approaches follows.

> **Identify and acknowledge feelings and beliefs.** Listen to the story to identify feelings expressed, and ask the storyteller to stop and name emotions he or she experienced. You might also inquire into tellers' emotions as they share the story; what does the telling evoke? As the storyteller names them, ask about those feelings and what the story means.
>
> If storytellers cannot or will not name their feelings, listeners can ask a question or make a statement that reflects what they believe those feelings are. Knowing he or she was heard may ease the teller's feelings. For example, Tim heard a man talk about the son he had disowned. Tim said to him, "It sounds as if you have tried to forget how much it hurts you to be separated from him." This reflection brought the man to the feeling dimension rather than staying stuck in his rationale, where he could only reiterate perceived misdeeds of his son.

Ask questions that redirect the storyteller's attention. Ask questions that help the storyteller see the situation from a different perspective.

For example, in the previous story the listener might ask, "How do you think your son sees this situation? Do you think he might have changed since you last talked?" The listener might also break the cycle of telling the story by asking, "What do you wish were different?" The answer will move the storyteller off the loop of the habitual story.

When dealing with difficult or traumatic situations, ask what the storyteller learned by overcoming or surviving the ordeal. Taking time to recognize the strength and courage the situation required in order to make it through the challenge provides deeper insight, understanding, and wisdom.

Afterword

Loving relationships are a privilege and a joy. Too often we miss opportunities to make the most of them. Our time on earth is limited, so we must take advantage of every moment to create and nurture the connections we have. We, the authors, hope this book has opened your mind and heart to what is possible with elders and dying loved ones, and demonstrated how to make that possibility a reality.

We have shared stories of people who took advantage of the opportunity to use Healing Conversations as a way to connect with loved ones, know them better, and enhance relationships. Many of the stories told of healing wounds and narrowing the distance between people. Sometimes they conveyed tales of aging well and finding acceptance of life as it is. Some stories dealt with those conversations that unite people when they recognize how limited time is after a serious diagnosis. They are all about creating fulfilling connections between people – those special, deeply meaningful connections we all yearn to experience.

We hope that the stories have created images of possibilities for you and your loved ones, so that you can imagine initiating Healing Conversations. We hope the questions, conversation starters, and suggestions for being present and listening in a connected way, increase your confidence to engage in Healing Conversations. We hope you have what you need in those situations so that you know what to say or do, and you can take the first, most difficult step.

It is our intention to make it possible to connect with those we long to touch and love more deeply. Let's make this a more loving world filled with caring relationships that heal the fundamental dis-ease, isolation, that too many experience.

For further support, to share your story or to hear others' stories, visit our website:

www.HealingConversationsNow.com.

You may also contact the authors directly at:

Joan Chadbourne at joan@HealingConversationsNow.com

Tony Silbert at tsilbert@HealingConversationsNow.com

Bibliography & Resource List

AGING & WELLBEING

Chittister, J., *The Gift of Years: Growing Older Gracefully.* BlueBridge. York, UK: 2001.

Cohen, G. D. Vintage Voices: The New Senior Moment. *Aging Well* (Winter 2008.).

Cohen, G. D. *The Creative Age: Awakening Human Potential in the Second Half of Life.* Quill. New York, NY: 2001.

Cohen, G. D. *The Mature Mind: The Positive Power of the Aging Brain.* Basic Books. New York, NY: 2005.

Gergen, M. and Gergen, K. J. Positive aging: New images for a new age, *Aging International Journal*, Vol. 27, No. 1 (December 2001) pages 3 – 23. Quoted in http://www.springerlink.com/content/un2x9hpgew1b0pt7/

Hill, R. D. *Seven Strategies for Positive Aging.* W. W. Norton & Company, London, UK: 2008

Lyubomirsky, S. *The How of Happiness: A Scientific Approach to Getting the Life You Want.* Penguin Press. New York, NY: 2008.

Lyubomirsky, S. L., Sousa, L., & Dickerhoof, R., The costs and benefits of writing, talking and thinking about life's triumphs and defeats. *Journal of Personality and Social Psychology,* Vol. 90:692-708. (2006) Cited in Lyubomirsky, *The How of Happiness,* page 315.

Schachter-Shalomi, Z. & Miller, R. S. *From Age-ing to Sage-ing: A profound New Vision of Growing Older.* Warner Books. New York, NY: 1995.

Smith R. "A good death." BMJ 320:129-130. 15 January 2000. 8 November 2006. http://www.bmj.com/cgi/content/full/320/7228/129 Debate of the Age, Health and Care Study Group. The future of health and care of older people: the best is yet to come. Age Concern. London, UK: 1999.

Bolte Taylor, J. *My Stroke of Insight.* Viking. New York, NY: 2006.

Thomas, W. *What Are Old People For? How Elders Will Save the World.* Vander Wyk & Burnham. Acton, MA: 2004.

Thomas, W. Maryland ProAging Event on YouTube, recorded at Erickson School at University of Maryland Baltimore Campus.

Vaillant, G.E. *Aging Well.* Little Brown and Company. NY: 2002.

DEATH & DYING

Byock, I. *The Four Things that Matter Most: A Book About Living.* Free Press: New York, NY: 2004.

Callanan, M. *Final Journeys: A Practical Guide for Bringing Care and Comfort at the End of Live.* Bantam Books. New York, NY: 2008.

Callanan, M. & Kelley, P. *Final Gifts: Understanding the Special Awareness, Needs, and Communications of the Dying.* Bantam Books. New York, NY: 1997.

Dowling S. K. *The Grace in Dying: A Message of Hope, Comfort, and Spiritual Transformation.* Harper. San Francisco, CA: 1998.

Gawande, Atul. Letting Go: What Should Medicine Do When It Can't Save Your Life? *The New Yorker.* (August 2, 2010): pages 36 – 49.

Kubler-Ross, E. *On Death and Dying.* Simon and Schuster, New York, NY: 1997

McNeil, D. Study Finds Palliative Care Extends Life, *New York Times.* August 18, 2010.

Meier, D. YouTube video, "What is Palliative Care?" *referenced in Frances Shani Parker's blog, Hospice and Nursing Home Blog's article, "Oncology Nurses, Cancer, and Palliative Care.* September 4, 2010

Neimeyer, R. A. *Lessons of Loss: A Guide to Coping. Center for the Study of Loss and Transition.* Memphis, TN: 2008.

Rusnak, K. *Because You've Never Died Before: Exploring The Spiritual World of the Dying.* 2010. Can be ordered at: www.Thebrickwall2.com

Rusnak, K. *Because You've Never Died Before: The World of the Dying. (2 CD Set)* Live second lecture with new and advanced material added, 2nd Edition 2005. Can be ordered at: www.Thebrickwall2.com

Sheehy, G. *Passages in Caregiving: Turning Chaos into Confidence.* Wm Morrow. New York, NY: 2010.

Kessler, D. *Visions, Trips, and Crowded Rooms: Who and What You See Before You Die.* Hay House, Carlsbad, CA: 2010.

APPRECIATIVE INQUIRY,
POSITIVE PSYCHOLOGY,
& SOCIAL CONSTRUCTIONISM

Cooperrider, D., & Barrett, F. *An Exploration of the Spiritual Heart of Human Science Inquiry.* Cleveland, OH: Case Western Reserve University, 2001.

Fredrickson, B. L. (2009). *Positivity: Groundbreaking research reveals how to embrace the hidden strength of positive emotions, overcome negativity, and thrive.* Crown. New York, NY: 2009.

Fredrickson, B. L. (2001). The role of positive emotions in positive psychology: The broaden-and-build theory of positive emotions. *American Psychologist*, 56, pages 218-226.

Fredrickson, B. L. (1998). What good are positive emotions? *Review of General Psychology*, 2, pages 300-319.

Gergen, K. J. *Relational Being: Beyond Self and Community.* Oxford University Press, New York, NY: 2009.

Gergen, K. J. & Gergen, M. *Social Construction: Entering the Dialogue.* Taos Institute Publications. Chagrin Falls, OH: 2004.

Kelm, J.B., *Appreciative Living: The Principles of Appreciative Inquiry in Personal Life.* Venet Publishers. Wake Forest, NC: 2005.

Lebow, G. & Kane, B. with Lebow, I. *Coping with Your Difficult Older Parent.* Avon Books. New York, NY: 1991.

Stavros, J. M. & Torres, C. B. *Dynamic Relationships: Unleashing the Power of Appreciative Inquiry in Daily Living.* Taos Institute Publications. Chagrin Falls, OH: 2005.

ENERGIZING QUESTIONS & STORYTELLING

Denning, S., *The Springboard: How Storytelling Ignites Action in Knowledge-Era Organizations.* Butterworth-Heinemann, Woburn, MA: 2001.

Dole, D., Hetzel Silbert, J., Mann, AJ, & Whitney, D. *Positive Family Dynamics: Appreciative Inquiry Questions to Bring Out the Best in Families.* Taos Institute Publications. Chagrin Falls, OH: 2008.

Lipman, D., *Improving Your Storytelling: Beyond the Basics for All Who Tell Stories in Work or Play.* August House Publishers, Inc. Little Rock, AR: 1999.

Simmons, A., *The Story Factor: Inspiration, Influence, and Persuasion through the Art of Storytelling.* Basic Books, New York, NY: 2002.

ONLINE RESOURCES

www.HealingConversationsNow.com - This website has additional questions and resources as well as a calendar of events.

www.changingaging.com - Dr. Bill Thomas's site that provides resources, thoughts and ideas for aging well.

http://dyingwell.org/ - Dr. Ira Byock's website which defines wellness through the end of life.

www.innovationpartners.com - Innovation Partners International is a consulting firm that specializes in appreciative approaches to organization design and change.

www.movinglifestories.com - Moving Life Stories captures the essence of life stories and documents them on DVD with music, photos, mementos and taped interviews.

www.thebrickwall2.com - Kathleen Rusnak's website about exploring the spiritual shift that emerges after a major crisis.

www.osher.net - Contains links to books, the LLI Review, and other information and resources about programs for seniors.

www.positiveaging.net - Positive Aging Newsletter. Edited by Ken and Mary Gergen, sponsored by the Taos Institute.

About the Authors

Joan W. Chadbourne, Ed.D. Joan has a doctorate in counseling psychology, was a professor, coach, and consultant in organizations in the US, Mexico, Europe, and Canada. The foundation of her professional work is appreciative. She was privileged to be present and discover pure love during her parents' dying times and years of special conversations with her elder aunts. This spiritual journey allowed her to experience the sacredness of connection and relationships. Combining professional and personal knowledge and experience she, with Tony, birthed Healing Conversations.

She now devotes full time to speaking, teaching, coaching, and writing about relationships, aging, dying, community, and the power of questions, stories and connected listening as described in *Healing Conversations Now*. She works with organizations that want to be people centered. She is a coach to those individuals addressing issues of aging and dying and is available to families who need support as loved ones are dying.

JOAN CAN BE REACHED AT:
joan@HealingConversationsNow.com
joanchad10@aol.com
Phone: 207-828-1339
Mobile: 207-232-5766
www.HealingConversationsNow.com

Tony Silbert, MSOD. Tony is a Principal of Innovation Partners International, and has over 20 years of experience in organizational development consulting, training, speaking, and facilitation. His areas of expertise include strengths-based and participatory approaches to change, strategy, innovation, and collaboration. Tony is Dean and faculty at National Training Laboratories (NTL), a Taos Institute Associate, and serves on the board of three local non-profits. He works with private, public and non-profit organizations both domestically and abroad. Tony is committed to positively transforming healthcare, elder care, and long-term care.

Tony's partnership with Joan and the birth of this book was prompted by powerful questions and conversations he had with his dying mother, Lynne (who passed of lung cancer in 2006). You can find Tony in South County, Rhode Island, where he lives, works, and plays with his wife and two young daughters.

TONY CAN BE REACHED AT:
tsilbert@HealingConversationsNow.com
tsilbert@InnovationPartners.com
Phone: 401-782-6131
Mobile: 401-787-2655
www.HealingConversationsNow.com
www.InnovationPartners.com

CPSIA information can be obtained at www.ICGtesting.com
263387BV00004B/1/P